Stable Rat

Stable Rat

Life in the Racing Stables

PHILIP WELSH

Eyre Methuen

First published in 1979
by Eyre Methuen Ltd
11 New Fetter Lane, London EC4P 4EE
Copyright © 1979 Philip Welsh
and Leigh Crutchley

British Library Cataloguing in Publication Data

Welsh, Philip
   Stable rat.
   1. Race horses – England – Epsom
   2. Epsom, Eng. – Stables
   I. Title
   636.1'2   SF335.5

   ISBN 0–413–45880–6

Photoset and printed
in Great Britain by
REDWOOD BURN LIMITED
Trowbridge & Esher

To my favourite punter
Leigh (Reggie) Crutchley

List of Illustrations

Acknowledgements are due to Rex Coleman, for Plates no. 5 and 8 b; to Central Press Photos Ltd for Plates 2 a and b, 3 c, 4 b, 7 a and b and 8 a; and to W. W. Rouch & Co. Ltd for Plates 3 a and b.

Preface

Since racing is very much a 'cap in hand' game, run on military lines, largely by retired officers, and since even today there is a censorship on what the rank and file may or may not say, it is perhaps only right that I offer some words of explanation for daring to write this book.

It is forty-seven years since as a lad I went into stables. Three years ago, when I was forcibly retired by the tax inspector who needed our stables to pay death duties, I was still a stable lad, still in the lowest rank, still sneeringly referred to as a 'stable rat'. Why then should I think that I have anything of interest or importance to add to what has already been written about racing?

My excuse is simple. Unlike those who have either inherited or risen to positions of importance, I have no image to preserve. I can 'tell the truth and shame the devil' as I was taught to do by my mother. By that I don't mean that I try to take the lid off racing, but that I am able to speak as I have found, and in that way present perhaps a truer picture than is usually given. That the picture is rough, sometimes crude, must be put down to the fact that I am what I am.

My main characters are the horses I have known, cared for and manipulated, the owners and trainers I've worked for, my colleagues the stable lads, and the various others who inhabit the racing world. I've enjoyed meeting them all, but the particular and permanent magnet has been my love of horses.

I look on myself only as the story-teller. I was one of many stable lads, and even though my tale is told autobiographically and to some extent chronologically, I've tried to push myself forward as little as possible.

That I have devoted more time to my early years is because through my training I inherited what had been the traditions and the standards of racing stables since racing began as a popular sport. It is only since the last war that major changes have taken place. Whether the changes have been for the better it is hard for me to judge. Another reason for my confining myself to this early period is the obvious one; I can write more freely about it without fear of any legal action.

Perhaps I should apologize that I have not written about the winning of classic races by glamorous horses. The kind of stables I worked in were run of the mill, but it is those and others like them that are in the majority, and it is through them that I believe the real story of racing can be told.

Finally, in attempting to be chronological, I have probably not always been as accurate with dates as some would like. Unfortunately in racing, we don't refer to the calendar, but to horses and races. 'That was the year Piggot won the Derby on Never Say Die', or nearer to home, 'When St Andrew II won the Brighton Autumn Cup in record time'.

Whether the book finds favour with others or not, I've enjoyed having written it, though I'd rather ride a villain in the National than start again. Through it I have been able to relive my life and to realize that I wouldn't wish it to have been any different and that I don't regret a minute of it.

I

*April fool – A fishmonger's son in South East London – Horses,
carts and traps – Billingsgate market – A holiday at Epsom –
Bitten by racehorses – Charlie Smirke lends a hand – Which
trainer, Wootten or Smythe? – A stable rat is born*

One thing about being born on April 1 is that no one forgets your
birthday. I could put up with my school mates calling me every
sort of a fool, at least they remembered and I was the centre of attention for one day a year. Even my teachers remembered and
although they might have made a sarcastic remark, which
brought a snigger from the rest of the class, I was never given the
stick on that day even if I deserved it.

I was a Great War baby. The year was 1916, the place Albert
Welsh's Fish Shop, North Cross Road, East Dulwich, SE22, in
the Peckham, Camberwell area of London. My father was home
on leave from the Army for the arrival of his first born, which
was just as well since someone had to run the shop while mum
was confined. Apparently dad behaved in the manner customary
to our class of family at the time; directly the doctor came down
and told him he had a son, he went off to spread the glad tidings
amongst his mates and got himself hit and missed in the process.
He returned to find an Indian salesman selling silks. Dad
grabbed one of the scarves and went upstairs to see mum and me.
He took me out of mum's arms and wrapped the scarf around
me. When he went down again, there was the Indian waiting for
his money. He asked dad a stupid price. He'd misjudged his man.
Drunk or sober, dad knew when he was being taken for a ride.
One look at my old man's face must have made him realise his
mistake because before dad pounced, he had shut his case and
was nearly out of the shop. But he was too late to avoid being
helped on his way by dad's boot. Dad and his kind didn't care

11

about the colour of the other man's skin, nor were they mean about money, it was just that they looked on any attempt to cheat them as an insult to their intelligence.

My schooldays at St John's Church School in our road were uneventful. I was no better and no worse than other boys of my class and age. I think we looked on schooling as a necessary evil. Our futures depended mostly on what our parents did. If you had a dad who was a navvy, you would probably be a navvy, to begin with at any rate. So it was taken for granted that I'd be a fishmonger and eventually inherit the shop. All I had to do was to be able to read, write and do arithmetic. What you didn't or wouldn't learn yourself was usually beaten into you. The cane was used as much as the blackboard and chalk. Women teachers were the worst, the most sadistic. Most women teachers were spinsters and it seemed they'd a grudge against males of any age. I expect it was because the world gave spinsters a hard time of it in those days. If that was the case you can't blame them. I was lucky that St John's was a church school. I got to know quite a bit of the Bible, which hasn't done me any harm at all, and we were given the religious holidays, some Saints' Days, Ash Wednesday and the like.

There was a glamour about London life at that time which spilled over into the suburbs, and it was free, free to join in or to look at. Perhaps I was lucky being born into the kind of family I was for it gave me a life that was as colourful, bright and glistening as a Christmas tree. The brightest light was, of course, my home, which was a sort of open house from eight in the morning until eleven at night, for by the time I was old enough to remember, dad had decided to go into frying fish on top of selling it wet and dry.

We knew everyone's affairs, mum and dad didn't look for the gossip, they had to listen, and in the process got to know what made the neighbourhood come alive. By the time I was eleven, I could have told you the name of every girl who was pregnant within a radius of half a mile, and who the father was, that is if the girls knew themselves. Then there were the street markets and the street traders and entertainers; the pubs on Friday and Saturday nights, the noise there was merciless. There'd be singing, shouting and later, of course, fighting. Young kids would be outside, some in prams, some lying around on the pavement,

12

some bawling for their mums and dads with no chance of being heard against all the noise inside.

Another light in my life was the horses. We kept as many as eight at one time for dad traded in them and hired them out as well. They were, of course, the smaller animals, not the shire horses, but they used to draw the carts and traps. We had a governess cart, the round barrel type, another trap with high wheels and springy shafts which we used on Sundays, and a couple of ordinary flat carts for carrying the fish back from market. I don't know when I learnt to ride or drive, I seem to be able to have done it since I can remember. The family's favourite horse was Dolly, a mare that generally pulled the fish cart to and from Billingsgate market. She was a real goer and I reckon dad lavished more affection on her than he did on the rest of the family.

Billingsgate market was to me the fairy on the Christmas tree. It wasn't until I was ten that mum allowed me to go there. I must say it meant more to me at the time than ever my twenty-first birthday did.

In a way I suppose I was lucky in that I had a good home, and there was always plenty of money. Not that I handled a lot of it. I was only given a penny a week pocket money, any extra I had to earn myself. After doing my stable work for dad, I found time to go on a paper round before school. Although we had money, mum and dad hadn't the time to enjoy it. We never took a family holiday, Sundays out was all I remember; a drive round Southend pond, Catford, or Hayes Common or a charabanc trip to Brighton on those wooden slatted seats, and being jolted around by every hole in the road, so that when you got there, you felt as though you'd been given six of the best. Sometimes we'd go to my Grandad and Grandma's, my mother's parents for Sunday tea. They lived in Stepney in the East End of London; we did the journey by tram. My grandfather was Irish, and Grandma Jewish. As my dad said, 'You could breed a Derby winner out of them two.' Much of their tea came off the barrows, there'd be motzas, beigels and muffins, and dad would buy winkles and shrimps on our way there. We didn't take our own from the shop, 'We've got to taste the opposition every now and then,' dad would say. Grandad was only a labourer, a brick maker, but he was a martinet. We children (I'd now two sisters and a brother)

13

had to sit quiet and bolt upright otherwise he'd shout at us like a sergeant major. He was the only man I knew who kept dad down. He'd sit there quiet as a lamb, yes sir, no sir, please sir, and I never heard him swear in that house. Mind you, he'd make up for it after we'd left, mostly at the old man's expense. I used to enjoy those visits, the grub was good and it made a change to see dad kept firmly in his place for an hour or two. I know mum felt the same way.

It goes without saying that the first smell I remember was of fish and you'd think it was something that today I would like to forget. You'd be wrong. I only wish I could find one of the old type of wet and dry shops with the fish laid out on the marble slabs as mum and dad did it in patterns, surrounded with chopped ice decorated with parsley and lemons, and surmounted by beautiful yellow brown smoked haddock, and grey smoked mackerel hanging from rods. Our shop used to look as colourful and neat as a garden by half-past eight in the morning. I still find it hard to pass a fish and chip shop, though I sometimes come out sneering at the way they're frying and the kind of fish they're using.

Dad had inherited our shop from his father. His two brothers were wholesalers in Blackpool, Fleetwood and Cleveleys. Some of their boxes came into Billingsgate, caught one day up north and sold the next down south. They were delivered by rail, never late and seldom were there any boxes missing or broken open. The wet fish would arrive packed in ice. We had a big slate bin in our yard, and regularly this would be filled by the London Ice Company, run by Eyties of course, from big vans that ran piddling along the streets. Huge blocks of ice they carried, but the men could cut them to any size needed with their expert handling of ice picks. They carried them from the vans through to the bin on their shoulders as easily as if they were giving a baby a piggy-back ride. Fishmongers worked continuously among ice. It didn't seem to do the hands much harm. Sometimes when they were unpacking, mum and dad had a bowl of hot water around so that when their hands went numb and blue with cold, they could plunge them into it and get the circulation back.

It was because of the lack of refrigeration that dad decided to go into the fish and chip business. He found it wasn't easy to judge the demand and any kind of wastage broke his heart, so fryers were installed. During the whole time I can remember the price was always the same, a penny for a bag of chips, threepence for a piece of fish, and twopence each for scallops. If the price of fish or potatoes changed in the market, then the customer got more or less for his money. Today, of course, fish and chips is one of the dearest things on the card.

One of my first jobs in the shop was cleaning the spuds. This I did in a large bucket with a bass broom, swilling them round and scrubbing them down. They weren't peeled, some of the skin came off in the cleaning; if it didn't, no one complained, it was supposed to be good for you. Our last customer every night was the constable on duty. The police station was opposite us on the corner of Upland Road. You could have thrown a piece of fish into it, so he had to come in carefully to avoid attention. He'd go into our sitting-room, put his helmet on the table and wait for whatever was left over to be brought in to him. If necessary dad would chuck a piece of fish or a handful of chips into the pan especially for him. There was no charge of course.

It was in exchange for an occasional bit of information, such as when the plain clothes men were likely to come round looking for prosecutions for selling after hours. 'Albert,' he'd say, 'Don't go selling anything after eight o'clock. The sergeant's having a stir up. There's two or three men come in from another station to go out on the prowl.' It was no good dad asking for a description of them, no one at the station knew them, except the super and perhaps the sergeant. Still, after they'd done a couple of shops, everyone knew who they were. But they were cunning. They'd stop kids in the street, give them money and ask them to go and buy, say, a quarter of a pound of bacon for them. That really riled dad, using children as decoys, so when a couple of days later they tried to get me to go and buy a pair of kippers from our shop at a quarter-past eight in the evening, I chucked the money back at them, ran off home and told mum and dad. Dad ran out of the shop, picking up a knife as he went, and made for the coppers. Mum was just as quick as she realized what he might do if he met up with them. She chased after him shouting at him to come back. But directly those plain clothes men saw him, they took to their heels. They knew they'd done the wrong thing and weren't prepared to take the consequences either from the magistrate or in particular from dad.

The weights and measures people dad treated more gently. He recognized that they had a job to do and that they went about it fairly. At one time he had a pair of scales with brass weights with the pieces of lead at the bottom to make sure they kept to the right amount. Some villains of shopkeepers would bang them around until this bit of lead fell out so that the customer would be an ounce or two short. I don't know whether dad ever did this. If so he never got caught, but I do know that directly the scales where the weight was shown by a needle came in, he bought one, and he went through that old rigmarole, 'Yes madam, you want a nice pair of 'addock fillets. They're eightpence, only eightpence a pound. Now you choose them yourself. You want that one? Yes,' he'd fling it on to the scales and the needle would start swinging, 'And that one madam.' He'd chuck the other one on, making the needle swing faster, and before it had stopped, he whipped the fish off, tossed it on a piece of paper, 'That'll be one and a tanner madam. Thank you very much. And the next please.' It would have been a bold customer who'd have challenged him. Mind you I don't think dad wanted to cheat. He didn't have to. To him it was just one of the tricks of the trade, part of the fun of being a shopkeeper. He was also a wizard at guessing weights. I never knew him to be more than an ounce out either way.

Dad knew the financial state of all of his customers. It wasn't just idle curiosity, it was his business to know. He spent quite a bit of his time in pubs and there he was what was known as an easy touch. People could spin him a yarn and if he swallowed it he was always good for up to a tenner. If ever he found he'd been caught for a sucker though, he was violent, and the fellow would never dare show his face to him again. In the shop and in the market, though, it was strictly business. He didn't expect credit and would rarely give it, if he did it was only a bob or two. He would, however, show a bit of sentiment. There'd be the dear old lady who dad knew had fallen on hard times, but who was too proud to admit it. She'd come along in her black serge suit that had got so threadbare with constant wear and brushing that it shone as though it had been polished with boot blacking. Her blouse would be clean and white, but frayed all round the seams, her gloves darned and her shoes stuffed with cardboard to try to keep the wet out. She'd wear a straw hat with a tired and faded flower drooping from it. 'Good morning, madam,' dad would greet her as if she were his most important customer. 'And what can I do for you this fine morning?' 'Oh good morning, Mr Welsh. I've just called to see if you have any bits for my cat.' Dad would point to the pile of coley and the like that he kept for the pets. 'Help yourself me dear,' he'd say. Then, removing her gloves, she'd search for the best bits. When she'd finished, dad'd pick up his knife and cut off a piece of cod. 'Let's give old Tom a treat today shall we?' 'Oh, thank you Mr Welsh, I'm sure he'll be very grateful,' would come the reply. They both knew it was all a pretence, but pride was so important to her. Charity was a dirty word. Once when she'd left the shop, some young codger was unwise enough to say, 'Bloomin' old moo, she don't want it for the cat, she wants it for herself.' Dad's fist moved like a piston. He went round the counter, lifted the poor beggar up by the collar and slung him out. 'Sod off, and don't come back. I don't serve the likes of you here.'

Dad knew that luck could change, not that I think his could have because he worked too hard. We had a smoke hole in the yard. He'd bring back five or six stone of haddock, four stone of herring from the market, gut them, split them, bone them and cut their heads off, then rack them and smoke them. Often he'd get out of bed at two in the morning to make sure that they'd reached the right colour. With haddock, it was that lovely golden yellow. They were never allowed to burn brown. These fish were all sold to hotels and restaurants, only a few were kept back for friends, special customers or ourselves. Shopkeepers in those days prepared their goods with love almost, taking a pride in every side of the job, nothing was too much trouble. If you didn't do your job properly, there were many others who did, and people would shop around, not just for price, but for quality, and if these weren't right in your shop, they were prepared to walk a mile to somewhere else where they were.

When I think back, I find it strange that none of our neighbours complained about the various smells that must have come from our place. Not that it would have got them anywhere, there was no planning permission needed, nor were there any rules about having extractor fans that shared the smells out over a wider area. I reckon if someone had complained to dad about it, he'd have told them to move elsewhere. In one way we did

17

consider our neighbours, that was in the storing and disposing of the fish offal. It was kept in the yard in big churns with tight fitting lids, and they had to be tight fitting to keep out the flies and bluebottles that swarmed around the smell of fish. Twice a week at around three in the morning a cart would call to collect. It had a great iron tank-like body with a manhole in the top, and through this the men would empty the churns. I don't know which was the worse, the stench from the cart or the smell from the men. Small wonder everyone slept with their windows shut when they knew the cart was calling.

Although the neighbours didn't mention the smell, they did go on a bit about the noise. I suppose they thought they could get away with it with dad, since it wasn't his fault, as he was at pains to tell them. 'Where there's muck there's money' must have been dad's motto, because he didn't give this offal away. It was collected and used by Pears, the soap people. 'Pears Glorious Golden Soap', the see-through tablet that was probably the best selling toilet soap at that time. I wonder how many people would have used it if they had known what it was made of.

There was one thing my childhood lacked — regular home-cooked meals. Mum and dad were both busy in the shop from first thing in the morning to last thing at night. I had to get my own breakfast, bread and jam and a cup of tea or milk. At lunch time there'd be the frying so I'd be given money to go to the nearest coffee shop, Charlie Thompson's. I'd either eat there or bring the meal back home between two plates. He let the plates leave the shop as they were so thick that everybody knew where they came from, so no one dared keep them. I got my own tea and if I was lucky mum would come out of the shop to get me a sort of scrap supper. I've often wondered if it was because of this irregular diet that I didn't grow much. I was never more than five foot-two in my socks. Still, a lot of cockney kids didn't grow so big in those days, and if I hadn't stayed small, I'd never have been able to go into the racing game.

I preferred staying for lunch at Charlie Thompson's. If I was around the house, I was at mum and dad's beck and call to run errands. I enjoyed the company at Charlie's. It was what was called a good pull-in for carmen, which was what the horse drivers were called. Although they might be only a couple of miles from home, they couldn't drive there at dinner-time like van drivers do today. They'd draw up outside the shop, put the nosebags on the horses, go into Charlie's without the bother of wiping their boots or washing their hands, and get a hot lunch and a cup of tea for a few pennies. Winter or summer it was always hot inside and on a wet day you wouldn't be able to see across the room for the smoke and the steam as their clothes dried on them. Dinner over, they'd pull out their papers, the *Sporting Life* or the '*Pink 'un*', contemplate their selections for the day, and then write out the betting slips. Before they drove off again, these would be handed to a bookie's runner through the back of their hands, with the money for the bets wrapped inside the paper. There would be a deal of glancing around to make sure the local bobby wasn't hanging about.

It was a right game of cops and robbers, rather like the way we behave today with traffic wardens when we feed the meters. The police spent a lot of their time chasing these runners, and the courts were often full of them, along with the daily parade of tarts. Both professions used to plead guilty and pay their fines with a bad grace. The bookies in our area, and I suppose it was the same in most parts of London, had the same kind of arrangement with the local bobby as dad had over selling after hours. The local coppers would pass the information on to the bookies in exchange for a few perks. Unlike dad, who could stop serving after hours for a few days without feeling the pinch, the bookies couldn't afford a single day's betting to go by without taking a penny, and they knew the police wouldn't let up until a few arrests had been made. They got round it though. Runners stood on certain street corners and they arranged it so that instead of the regulars operating, they employed men who were out of work and needed a quid or two, and who had a clean police record, to take their places and to make themselves as obvious as possible without giving the game away. They'd be quickly hauled off to the station and while that was happening, the regulars would move in and collect to their hearts' content. The following day, the decoys would appear in court, and get fined five bob, since their slates were clean. The fines were paid by the bookies and everybody was happy for a few weeks.

Though nothing is ever perfect, I had a good home life. Dad's drinking was the only fly in the ointment. He wasn't an alcoholic, just a hard and heavy drinker and while sometimes it made him happy, and fun to be with, at others he became mean and violent, and like most working-class men who got into that condition, he took it out on his missus. Mum took it philosophically, as women had to, and of course when he sobered up, dad would be all apologies, but to me and my brother and sisters, it was frightening when it happened. There's a saying that some good comes out of everything and I'm certain that it was my dad's behaviour that made me swear as a kid I'd never let drink get the better of me. It only did once when some mates and I looted wine in Italy during the war. It didn't make me or the others belligerent, I just passed out cold. When I came to and opened my eyes, the place looked like a battlefield, with ten corpses lying round a couple of tanks. We'd all just sparked out.

It was because of dad's fondness for the bottle that at the age of ten I was allowed to go with him to Billingsgate market on Saturdays and holidays. Mum thought Saturday was one of dad's bad days, and she worried about him driving back home half cut. For the uninformed, the pubs around Billingsgate opened with the market. I don't know whether I was the guardian angel mum expected me to be, but sometimes dad would be singing and cheering all the way home. At other times he'd pass the reins over to me, and sit snoring in the back of the cart. I don't think there was an age limit for driving then, or know whether there is now. Anyway I was never stopped, but that may have been because anyone could see that I knew what I was doing. It seems too hard to believe that only fifty years ago you could drive a horse and cart from East Dulwich, down Rye Lane Peckham, Peckham Park Road, Glengarry Road, Sumner Road and along the Old Kent Road and across Tower Bridge to Billingsgate without any real traffic worries. Dad loved horses, and as we drove along he'd be weighing others up and comparing them. 'I wouldn't mind being behind that, would you Phil?' he'd say, in much the same way that people admire a Rolls or a Jaguar today.

Once we got to the market, we'd find a place to park on Tower Hill. There was a bloke there called Charlie, whose job it was to look after the horses and carts. He'd tether us and give us a number on a metal disc. This was important because when you'd bought your fish, you'd give the number to the porter or bummaree, as he was called, and he'd carry the boxes and load them on the cart. Mostly he'd take them on his head. There was a special sort of leather cap they wore to carry them on. Only if it was a really heavy load would he use a truck. Great strong fellows these bumarees were. Little wonder that many of our best boxers came from their ranks. To me as a lad they were an example of everything that was British and best; strong, fearless, proud and independent. It's many years since I've been to Billingsgate, but I wouldn't mind betting they're the same now.

Particularly I used to enjoy the buying. First, when I went there, the fishmongers would greet dad, then look down at me and say 'And oo's this? Is this yourn Albert? Mmm good looking lad. What's your name son?' 'Phil. Good to meet you Phil, let's hope you'll turn out as good as your old man, eh Albert.' This was said to butter dad up of course. ''ere Phil, I expect you'll know what to do with this' and they'd hand me a tanner or a bob.

After the buying was over, it was always the same old tale. 'Well now lad,' dad would say 'I expect you're 'ungry. 'ere's a tanner, go and get yourself some breakfast. I got business to attend to', and off he'd go to the pub, while I made my way to what passed there for a coffee shop. It was an old railway carriage set on bricks but it served its purpose. Even on the coldest day it was as cosy as a bug in a rug. There was one of those round iron fires in the middle with a pipe going through the roof and it was stoked up so that it was generally nearly red-hot. My order was always the same 'Two of drip and a cuppa.' This was two thick slices of toast with dripping and a mug of tea. It was even more fun among the fish blokes than with the cart men. They seemed to have more to talk about, and like the dripping their conversations was liberally spiced. Their language was strong and I soon discovered that what was said about the fish wives was absolutely true. The men used to rile them purposely. A couple of women would come in. ''allo me old darlings' they'd greet them and then they'd make some reference to certain portions of their anatomy. This started it. It was as if the women knew what was expected of them and did it as a sort of party piece, or maybe they knew they were 'singing for their supper' because when the abuse had begun to die down, one of the blokes would say, 'All right luvs, no 'ard feelings. Come on, what are you going to 'ave?' Then he'd shout across to whoever was serving, 'Down to me guv'ner' and it was all forgive and forget. I didn't catch the

21

swearing habit, well not all that much anyway. It would have been as much as my life was worth to have used such words at home in front of mum.

Waiting for dad to drink his fill wasn't all milk and honey. The staff of the coffee shop were good to me and would let me sit there long after I'd finished my tea, but some mornings there would be customers waiting for a seat and I'd have to leave and go to the cart. Sometimes I served mum's purpose. I'd get so cold that I'd have to go round to the pub to remind dad of my existence. Give him his due, it usually worked. I think it was that he didn't want to get a bad name with his mates. If I thought he might create, I'd tell him the horse was getting a bit restive. That always did the trick. He was fond of his horses was dad.

It was while I was still at home that I had my first introduction to a thoroughbred horse. Around 1927 dad got bitten by the pony trotting bug and regularly on Sunday mornings we'd drive the trap over to the meeting at Greenford in Essex. It was near where Northolt airport is now. Dad was a member of the club, enjoyed drinking there and having a bet with his mates. Though trotting has never taken on over here, it's a very popular sport in Australia and the States even today. The ponies pull a sulky, a two wheeled carriage for one driver. It's a light, flimsy, bi-cycle-framed affair, not too easy to manoeuvre. The pony is only allowed to trot. If it breaks into a canter it's disqualified. Trotting is a pretty and graceful motion. The pony's legs swing two one side and two the other, while an ordinary horse moves corner to corner.

One Sunday dad and his cronies started boasting about their prowess with horses and the conversation came round to driving a sulky. Dad announced he was sure he could beat any of the present company driving one and the challenge was taken up. Of course dad hadn't got a pony or a sulky but one of his pals offered to lend him his. It was decided that the odds against dad winning were two to one. To show his confidence dad wagered twenty quid. It was just as well I was the only member of the family there because if mum had got to hear of it she would have gone ber-serk. I must say as I watched dad get up on that sulky I was a bit windy. If he hurt himself I should be partly to blame in mum's eyes. Then again I had a feeling that dad was going to make a fool of himself and I didn't care for the idea of that. I'd always been proud of him. But I was wrong on both counts. He didn't win easily, by a neck I think it was, but he drove as good a race as any did that day. I'd never seen him so pleased with himself and to give the punters their due, they were happy for him. The drinks came thick and fast and I began wondering whether his victory had been such a good thing after all. Suddenly out of the blue, the owner of the pony asked dad if he'd like to buy it. He'd chosen his moment right. 'Buy him?' said dad ''ow much?' 'Thirty quid.' 'Done,' said dad, and so we became the owner of a gelding pony called Clinch Fast.

We must have looked like a couple of gypsies taking Clinch Fast home with dad driving the trap and me in the back holding the horse on a halter. Dad was crowing like a cockerel all the way. 'We showed 'em, didn't we Phil?' although for the life of me I couldn't see what part I played in it all. Naturally he was eager for mum to see the pony. She wasn't too pleased at first, a bit suspicious ''ow did you get 'im and what did 'e cost?' she asked. 'I won 'im in a competition, didn't I Phil?' dad announced triumphantly and when I agreed, mum seemed more happy. 'What are you going to do with him?' 'Drive 'im to market of course.' He waited until the following Saturday because he wanted me to go with him, 'Just in case things go wrong,' he told me. I must say Clinch Fast was as good as gold.

On the return journey, however, dad had to pick up the whip and clip the horse a couple of times around the arse. Clinch Fast took off like a rocket. I landed on my back among the boxes of fish and as I regained my balance, I saw that sparks were flying everywhere and could hear that the jeers had turned to cheers, with dad's pals now joined by the passers-by hallooing us on our way. We got up Tower Hill in record time and careered round the Tower of London. Although dad had the reins in his hands, it was clear to me that he had no control of the horse. Then I saw Tower Bridge, and my belly gave a lurch: 'What if it starts opening just as we get on it,' I thought. In those days the Port of London was busy and traffic across the bridge was forever being held up while the ships went through. And there were no safety devices, just an old geezer who raised a red flag to stop the traffic and a bell ringing in one of the towers, and the way Clinch Fast was going, he wouldn't be stopping for any bell or flag. I could see us driving through the bridge just as it was rising and either being shot into the Thames or pitched backwards and landing arse over tip on the run up to the bridge. But Lady Luck was with us. The bridge stayed put and we flashed over it.

As we were going up the Old Kent Road, the pony began to tire, and at last dad was able to make his own strength tell. He looked down at me, 'Christ Phil, let's 'ope we don't have to go through that again.' His face looked a bit pale and drawn. Mine must have been the same because he put his arm round my shoulder and patted me on the back. 'Good lad,' he said. It was the only time I think I ever saw him display fear or affection.

It was when I was thirteen that events decided my future. It was Derby Sunday, that is the Sunday before Derby week, a day when all the working-class people did their best to get on Epsom Downs to join in the fun of the fair, mix with the gypsies, the tricksters, the tipsters, the pearlies or just to get the smell of smoke out of their nostrils by picnicking in the country air among people of their own kind. It was the sort of day when Jack would feel as good as his master. He looked on Epsom as his own race course and he liked to see it at least once a year. Like everyone else, our family dressed up flash and drove there in the governess cart. We went to the middle of the course, took Dolly out of the shafts, tied her to the wheel and while she munched away at the grass, we all set out to enjoy ourselves, meeting up again for tea. Mum hadn't brought anything, so she and dad went to get what we wanted from a small tea tent. There they met Mrs Dodd, who at one time had lived just down the road from us. She and her husband had bought a bungalow in Epsom at Langley Vale, ran it as a sweetshop and on race days had this tent on the Downs. Apparently she particularly remembered me. 'She'd like to see you again,' mum said, 'I'll take you to meet her when we've 'ad our tea.' I groaned inwardly, it was the sort of thing I hated, being taken along and put on show. But to my surprise and delight Mrs Dodd said, 'How would you like to come and spend some of your next holiday with us Phil? You'd have to earn your keep but it'll make a change for you.' I jumped at the idea, so did mum and dad and it was all arranged then and there.

I went to stay with Mrs Dodd for the first week of my summer holidays and the days weren't long enough. I explored the Downs, was up every morning watching the gallops, served in the shop, ran errands and got to know some of the local characters. I collected water from the spring at the bottom of Rosebery Vale, there wasn't even cold water laid on in the houses around, and no roads only cart tracks; on Sunday I picked the watercress from the stream which ran from the spring.

Percy Allden, the trainer who later moved to Newmarket, had his stables nearby. I even remember a two-year-old he had by the name of Knighted. He was a real goodun and won many races. I'd watch him and others as they cantered on the tan track, about two-and-a-half furlongs of oak tan put down to a depth of about eight inches. It was the first part of their exercise, or so I learned from his stable lads who were friendly, anxious to talk and proud of their animals. I liked the place, I liked the people, but most of all I liked the horses.

When I went back home and told them about it, my enthusiasm must have showed. 'Never known Phil so talkative, nor looking so well and happy,' mum said, which must have meant something, because I'd always been outgoing, with my tongue forever rattling. One morning as dad and I were driving back from market he said, 'What 'appened to you at Epsom Phil? You've bin as fidgety as a sore-arsed monkey since you came back. Did you find yourself a bit of skirt or something?' He didn't think it of course, it was his way of probing. It gave me my chance. 'No dad,' I said straight out, 'It's just that it got me fancying to be a jockey.' It took some courage for me to tell him, I thought that he'd either laugh at me or be angry that I didn't want to take over the shop from him. He looked at me sharply, 'You mean it lad?'. 'Yes, dad, I do,' I said. 'Well, we'll have to see what we can do about it.' I was bowled over, for if my old man spoke like that, it meant he would do something, and such was my faith in him, that I could already see myself in the winning enclosure.

Nothing more was said for a few days, then one evening dad announced that on the next Sunday mum, he and I were going down to Littlehampton, 'To see me old pal Charlie Smirke,' dad added with a wink at me. Old Charlie Smirke had, until recently, been a fishmonger in the Old Kent Road. He was a Cockney born and bred; Cheeky Charlie they used to call him. His wife, Alice, was the same, as Cockney as no one has made them since, she could swear and curse, but at heart she was the greatest woman you could ever meet. Charlie had sold up his shop, moved down to Littlehampton, bought himself a house and a barrow and started a successful fish round. Old Charlie had a son of the same name who had been apprenticed to Stanley Wootten and had become one of the best jockeys of his day. He also had another boy Alfie, who'd just joined Wootten.

When the Sunday came, we made our way to Victoria by tram. Our two-and-a-half day return tickets to Littlehampton cost twelve and a tanner. Charlie's house was only a stone's throw from the station. It was one of a row of terraced houses alongside the railway line, and backing onto a recreation ground; 'Can't be built on behind,' he said to us proudly as we were being shown over. Dad played cool about me wanting to be a jockey. 'We won't rush it,' he said. 'We don't want Charlie thinking that's the reason for us coming down, nor do we want it to look as if he's doing us a big favour. We'll let him bring it up and then just leave the talking to me.'

After the meal while the women cleared away and washed up, dad steered the conversation round to me. Old Charlie took the bait. 'What do you want to do when you leave school, Phil?' 'I'd like it to be something to do with horses, get myself into some stables, Mr Smirke,' I replied as I had been told. Dad's instructions had been 'Don't just say you want to be a jockey straight out, Phil, he might laugh you out of it.' 'Fancy yourself as a jockey like my boys?' 'Well yes, sir.' I said. From then on dad took over. I think in a way Charlie wanted to show dad that he had some influence in such matters. 'Tell you what, Albert, next Sunday we'll meet in Epsom and I'll take you to see my friend Stanley Wootten. He'll be able to tell if the boy's got it in 'im and 'e'll take 'im on if he thinks he has, you mark my words.'

The week passed too slowly for my liking, but when Sunday came I felt dreadful, and I thought I looked it. Mum had bought me a new suit with long trousers, the first time I'd worn them. It was a city type of suit, I knew it was, not the sort of things a boy going into stables would be wearing. We drove down to Epsom in the trap, picked Charlie up at the station as arranged and arrived bang on eleven at Stanley Wootten's house, Shifnal Cottage. It was a beautiful place, backing on one of his yards. He had another bigger yard at Treadwell House. The cottage door was opened by a man servant, and he showed us into the sitting-room.

By now, small though I was, I was feeling knee high to a grasshopper. Stanley Wootten was a great trainer, he had had some brilliant horses through his hands, and trained many good jockeys. People like Les Cordell, Arthur Wragg, Snowy Carrol, Frenchy Nicholson, Frankie Fields, Monkey Morris, father of Dean Morris who recently retired as a jockey, as well of course as Charlie Smirke. Introductions were made, then Mr Wootten turned to me. He was as great a gentleman as he was a trainer, and soon put me at my ease. Then he told me to take my jacket off and roll my sleeves up. He was like a doctor examining a patient. 'Now turn up your trousers.' I blessed mum and the drainpipes. He felt my thighs and calves. 'Well he's not large-boned, though he may get a bit heavy later on,' he said, and then paused for a bit. 'Look,' he said 'I' want to be fair to you. I'll take him, but I must warn you I've already got a dozen apprentices on my staff, most of them gooduns. Your boy will be at the end of the queue and unless he shows exceptional ability he'll stay there. My advice is to go to another trainer who'll most likely be able to give him a quicker opportunity.'

This put dad and Charlie back on their heels a bit, got them humming and ha-ing. Charlie was all for settling with Wootten, but dad played it carefully. 'Is there anyone you can recommend sir, that might give him a chance?' I think it pleased Mr Wootten that he had taken notice of his advice. 'Yes,' he said 'Herbert Smythe is a bit short-staffed. He's a good man, and your boy would do well with him I'm sure. If you like, I'll have a word with him on the phone.' Dad said he'd like that. Mr Wootten left the room and returned a couple of minutes later with the news that Herbert Smythe would see us. He looked at his watch 'You'll have to hurry though,' he said with a smile, 'he takes a drink on a Sunday, and the pubs will soon be open.'

We could only have missed him by a short head. The maid told us Mr Smythe was in the Derby Arms. Neither dad nor Charlie needed telling where that was so off we trooped and I was told to sit at a table outside. Charlie knew Herbert well, so they quickly made their way over to a group of men drinking pints. Charlie introduced dad and reminded him of the conversation with Wootten. 'You'll have to wait until the pub shuts' Herbert said briefly, 'I never discuss business during opening hours on Sundays.' Dad came outside with a lemonade and a Brighton biscuit

27

for me and told me the news. He didn't seem at all put out at the delay. As I watched from the garden, drink following drink, I began worrying, 'No one's going to be in any position to talk about anything.'

I'm glad to say I'd underestimated dad, for when he came out, he looked as fresh as a daisy, so did Charlie and Herbert Smythe. Together we went round to Mr Smythe's house and I was put through the same examination as at Stanley Wootten's. Herbert's words, though, were more encouraging. 'I'll tell you what I'll do, I'll give the lad a fortnight's trial. If I think he's going to make the grade, 'e can stay, and if he continues promising, I'll eventually take 'im on as an apprentice. 'ow's that suit yer?' Dad and Herbert Smythe shook hands on me while I stood there with my trousers rolled up. I was going to be a stable rat. The bells were ringing in my head. I was in the race, I'd jumped my first fence, I was certain I could finish the course and I did, but it was a blooming rough ride.

2

Moving in — 'Auntie' Kildare: landlady or prison warder? — Less than the chaff — 'Learning' to ride — My first horse — Sandown: the Military Gold Cup — Hurdles and fences — Stable routine — 'A good stable lad is the best horse in his governor's stables'

I think that when he said he would take me on a fortnight's trial, Herbert Smythe was playing hard to get. All I did for those two weeks was hang around, watch the other lads at their stable routines, fetch and carry for them, run any errands for the house and generally act as a dogsbody. The only thing Herbert, or Nat as many of his friends called him, could have found out about me was that I could get up in the morning and be at work by six o'clock and that I wasn't afraid of getting in amongst the horses. Mum came to Epsom to see what her son was letting himself in for. She met the governor and pronounced her verdict, ''e seems a nice enough man. A bit gruff perhaps, but at the back of 'im, he's soft. I don't think he'll be cruel to yer.' I liked the stable lads, who were proud of their horses and seemed anxious to talk about them. Their general opinion of Herbert was that he was a hard bugger but fair, and a good man to be working for. When I told them what mum had said, they didn't agree about him being part soft, or at least they'd never found him so. It must have been a quality he only allowed to show to members of the opposite sex.

At the end of my trial period, Herbert sent for me. 'Well, Phillup,' as he used to call me, as though he was asking for his beer glass to be filled. 'It looks like you're lucky. I'm willing to take yer on regular, and if you work hard, and behave yourself I might one day make you an apprentice. But remember you're here to bloody learn, and if you do, when you leave me, you'll be able to get a job anywhere and do anything.' When he said it I thought he meant do anything with horses. He didn't. While I was with him I learnt carpentry, painting, bricklaying, gardening and straightforward navvying. The other lads and I cursed him for a slave driver, but it has served every one of us well since. What stopped us complaining more than we did was that two of his sons, Ted and Ron, were apprentices at the time, as later was his youngest son, Tony, and if anything he treated them harder than he did us.

The governor then went on to say that my money would be half-a-crown a week, but that he would pay my landlady for board and lodging, provide my stable gear, pay my insurance and any doctor's bills – he obviously hated the bills. 'There's one other thing, Philup,' he went on, 'that's your schooling. You're only thirteen-and-a-half so you've got six more months to go. I've had a word with the headmaster here and he's agreed to you having a tutor.' Here he winked at me. 'So I've arranged with my pal, Bert Childs, that he'll give you a few private lessons from time to time.' I took his meaning. Bert Childs was a drinking companion. These lessons were very enjoyable compared with what I'd been used to. I learned arithmetic by working out bookmaker and totalisator odds, measurements in hands, short heads, heads, lengths and furlongs, and weights through handicaps, bales of hay and sacks of corn! He taught me reading through the racing pages of the daily papers, so that I got to know the various horses. He also lent me books that were nothing to do with racing and I learned how to enjoy those. With these methods he caught my interest and I believe I owe Mr Childs a great deal. Finally, Herbert told me to go back to Mrs Dodd's to pack and he would take me down and introduce me to my future landlady. I had to live with someone who was known in the game and who would account for me to my trainer.

When I came back with my little nanny-bag, we set off. On the way he gave me some idea of what to expect. 'They're comfortable lodgings and the grub's good, but Ma Kildare is a bit of an old sod. She'll look after you, but she won't let you mess her about so it's no good you running to her apron strings. She'll treat you rough and ready, but she has a reputation of being a good woman with kids.' Mrs Kildare lived at 17 Treadwell Road. From the abrupt way Herbert introduced me and quickly disappeared, I got the impression that he was a bit scared of her. She didn't waste much time in making my position clear, for I'd hardly put my bag down when she started in on me. 'I make the rules around here,' she began. 'If you abide by them, well and good, we'll all be happy. If you don't you'll soon know what to expect.' She told me the meal times. 'That's when the food is on the table. If you're here, you'll eat it, every scrap of it. If you're not, you'll go hungry. You'll be in at night before ten o'clock. You'll leave your boots outside in the scullery and you'll clean them before you go to bed. You'll write home twice a week and you'll hand the letters for me to post. I'm not having your mum and dad worrying about you. You'll keep a civil tongue in your head and use no bad language, no matter what you may hear John or I say,' (John was her husband). 'You'll wash regular and I'll know because you'll do it in the sink here. Friday nights is bath nights and you'll change your things on Saturday morning, leaving the dirty ones in a neat pile for me to wash. Is all that understood?' I nodded. I didn't feel I was called upon to answer. She then took me upstairs to see my room and the bed I was to share with Manch, her nephew, for the next nine years. Manch was A. P. Taylor who later became first jockey to Vernon Hobbs of Lambourne, and ended up as a trainer. She left me alone to unpack and I started wondering what I'd let myself in for. It seemed the place was going to be more like a prison than a home. But rough diamond she may have been, and many's the rollocking I had from her, but she was a second mother to me and I have more to thank her for than she ever knew.

She was as good as her word. She watched me like a hawk for the first few weeks. She was most particular about my cleanliness. Manch always had first bath. I don't know whether she thought I was jealous, anyway one day she drew attention to it. ''e gets it first because he's my nephew, and blood is thicker than water, even this bloody dirty stuff.' After I'd been there a month or two, with Manch always referring to her as Auntie, I fell into the habit. She and John didn't have any children and she guarded over us as if we were her own. If there was any trouble in the area from stable lads, we'd hear her say 'My boys wouldn't do anything like that,' and woe betide anybody who said we had. I remember a neighbour coming to complain when we'd pinched apples off his tree. 'Must be some mistake,' she said to him, 'my boys wouldn't do that.' Then she shut the door in his face and went back to peeling the apples we'd brought in for her earlier in the day.

Mum and dad thought the world of her and John, and brought them a cotchall of fish whenever they visited. This pleased Auntie no end, and whenever I got a letter from home, she'd straight away ask when they were coming down again. Herbert Smythe was the same, though he used to tell me what he wanted. It was either sole or 'one of them big haddocks that your dad smokes himself'. Although mum knew that a sort of special relationship had developed between myself and the Kildares, she wasn't the least jealous. Whenever I went home for a visit, her last words before I left would be, 'Now make sure you do whatever Auntie tells you, that way I'll know you're keeping out of trouble.' It was getting back in time at nights that was the hardest, particularly if Manch and I had been going out after girls. We'd say that we'd been to the pictures, but Auntie would ask us what the film was about. We got cunning though, and before going on a prowl we'd find out from the other lads what the plot was, and some of the finer points of the film.

Like most of the people in Epsom, Auntie was one for the horses, and she got some good information. Either Manch or I would have to place the money for her. This wasn't so tricky as it would have been in London since the police turned a blind eye as much as they could, and if a runner did get caught, the magistrates were lenient. It was the same in any racing town, dog didn't eat dog. Joe Cliff was our local bookie. He had an arrangement with a nearby bootmaker and cobbler, Dukey Hawtin, to take his bets. When we went into his shop, there would be a pair of boots standing on the counter. We'd pass the time of day with Dukey, at the same time stuffing the slips and the money into a boot. It worked to everyone's satisfaction for years, then someone blew the gaff and the police had to move in.

Eventually I got married from Aunties and she gave me a right send off. After John died I visited her regularly, then she developed diabetes and to her great distress had to stop drinking beer or stout. Still she had an understanding doctor who allowed her to drink Jamesons, the Irish whisky. I know Dermot Whelan, who now trains at Epsom, kept her well supplied, as did many others. When Auntie died she left me all her belongings, but it didn't seem right for me to have them, so I handed them over to her brother. I reckon the dozen or so bottles of Jamesons we found in her cupboard were as good an epitaph as any.

From the word go I hit it off with Manch Taylor. He'd already been with Smythe a few months before I joined and so knew the ropes. He was a first-class horseman which helped when we were riding out, particularly if I was on a frisky one, for some of the lads would then ride up close behind me, half hoping that my horse would set alight and go. I'd only have to shout 'Get off my arse,' and Manch would quietly push his mount in between them and shear them away. Again, if I was leading and my horse started playing up, he'd move alongside, which would generally steady it. As we grew up together, we became closer, sharing secrets and ambitions as well as indulging in mischievous, sometimes downright bad behaviour.

Once I was on the regular staff as an assistant, everyone's attitude towards me hardened. I was now the lowest of the low, someone to be used or misused as the occasion arose. If I expected sympathy from Manch I was unlucky. For some reason or other if people have been given a hard time of it themselves, they think it's right and proper that the same thing should happen to you. I suppose it was my attitude later, but it didn't make things better at the time. Manch did give me some ray of hope. 'You'll find it easier when Herbert gives you your first horse.' At the time I was looking after an old hack. I supposed there was some kind of snobbery amongst the lads – you were treated as contemptuously as the horse you were doing over.

Eventually what Manch had forecast proved to be right. I was given a horse and the lads began to let up on me a bit. In the meantime, Herbert had been teaching me to ride. With my previous experience I thought that I would surprise him with my ability. I was soon put in my place. 'The trouble with you, Phillup, is that you think you can ride, when you can't even sit on a bloody horse properly. It's going to be worse teaching you than a rookie. You've got bad habits, and you're going to have to forget them before you start to learn.' So it went on, every lesson was one long shout, and when eventually I was allowed to ride out, it was the same. He followed behind me bellowing every two seconds. Whether it was the right or wrong way of learning I shall never really know. It was the only way Herbert knew of teaching. I do know that he made me think and concentrate until it came natural to me.

Time Enough was my first horse. She was an old mare of thirteen who'd been a jumper, was then at stud, had one foal and gone barren. She belonged to a Mr Usher, an amateur rider, who decided she was still young enough to be able to ride, so he put her back in training. When she arrived she looked a real scraggy old animal. I was standing near the horsebox and the governor called out to me, 'Here's one for you to do Philup, you can look after her, she'll just suit you. She knows more about the game than you do and she'll teach yer.' I thought he was joking but he wasn't. By the time she'd been clipped, physicked, wormed and well fed to put weight on her she looked a different animal. She was a big old horse, and I had to stand on a box when I did her quarters, a quiet, motherly old thing who had become more tender through having a foal. If I did anything that she didn't like, she wouldn't kick out or rear up. She'd look at me, as much as to say 'Don't do that again, please.' I remember one day, Herbert was watching me, I did something wrong, and she gave me one of her looks. 'It's like I told you Philup,' he said, 'if you're not sure, ask her, she'll tell you.' It was enjoyable riding her out. She was so quiet I could relax and chat to the other lads.

One day as we were leaving stables, the governor rode up to me and said, 'Do you think you could ride her a mile and a half, Philup?' Naturally I said yes. 'Right then, you go with Tom Carney, Paddy Connolly and Jack Hanks.' They were three of our heavier lads that were experienced jumpers. 'You'll take the horses down by the back of the Derby start, into Langley Vale, to the mile and a half post, and I'll be waiting for you at the finish.' It was the long way round so we didn't have a chance of seeing the gallop. We set off at a fair pace, with me in the middle, so that the other lads could look after me. When we approached the mile, I was so busy concentrating on holding the mare, who had a habit of racing with her head down, that I wasn't really looking in front. Suddenly one of the lads called out 'Quick, pull up, the gallop's shut.' By the time this had sunk in and I looked up, it was too late. There were the iron railings in front of us. I couldn't turn as the others had and I was too near to pull up. I did the only thing left to me, shut my eyes, prayed and waited for the crash. It didn't come. Instead I went sailing into the air as the old mare jumped the bar as clean as a whistle. By some miracle I landed back in the saddle, I was nearly unshipped but managed to recover. The mare took over for the next furlong, but I was able to get control of her before I reached the finish, and Herbert Smythe. 'What the bloody hell's happened to you? Where are the rest? Couldn't you hold her?' As I started to tell him, the other lads rode up. 'The kid jumped the bloody railings at the mile post like a real goodun,' and the story came out. The governor examined the horse. 'She seems all right, but you look a bit white round the gills Philup.' I bit my tongue hard so as not to tell him that he'd look the same if he'd just done what I had. 'Oh, I'm O.K.' I said, offhand, as if I was used to jumping such obstacles every day. For once the old man was at a loss for words, he grunted and rode off. I was a bit of a hero among the lads for a day or two, and I saw to it that Time Enough got a few tasty extras, for I reckoned she'd saved my life, or at any rate my racing career.

It was a pity the old mare didn't win any races, but she didn't disgrace herself. I had to get her ready for the Military Gold Cup at Sandown. It was a famous race in those days. It's still run today, but it's not the same. It was then the Army equivalent to the Grand National and it was an honour to ride in it. Cavalry regiments still had their horses as did many officers in the regiments of the line. The riders would dress in their colours long before the race and strut around like peacocks with their ladies, or in order to impress others. Like the National, it was something to complete the course, for Sandown Park was very stiff country to jump at that time. Fences were built as fences. No one went round to tell you how high they had to be or what shape, no one made sure that the guard rails were painted to encourage the horses to jump. They weren't encouraged. Some of the fences were natural growing – blackthorn. Beecher's Brook at Aintree was one which had been growing there for years. Gatwick was notorious for its fences. The wartime Nationals were run there. The water jump was built of concrete, three inches all the way round to hold the water. Now they're made of soil lined with clay and the water seeps out overnight. Building fences was an art that was passed down from foreman to foreman over generations before the inspectors were brought in to regulate everything with the motto of safety first uppermost in their minds and to insist on 'dandy-brush' fences, a term of contempt with the old hands.

Every course had some particularly difficult obstacle. I've seen tough experienced jockeys pale when they've been told they were riding at Ludlow. Aintree was always the hardest ride, but with it went the greatest honour. It was said of the men that built the course that they did it with the object of having no horses finish, and that their ambition was to make a fence no horse could jump. The element of risk was what it was all about. Even hurdle races were more hazardous. Today the hurdles are sloped so that if a horse hits one, he knocks it on to the ground, but in my day they were straight, driven into the earth up to the bottom rail, so that if you hit them, they swung back at you nine times out of ten. This is why when you get a crowd of older racing men together, you hear them talking in awe of steeple chasers and their jockeys of yesteryear, it's more like old soldiers talking about the battles, real battles, fought under hard conditions, when both the horses and the men were heroes.

I'm not blaming the racing fraternity for these changes. Some of them may have been necessary, but most of them have been brought about by people who've never been on a race course, and who don't know the first thing about racing men, or real horses. I believe any man worth his salt needs to test himself to pit his wits, his strength and his courage against the odds, and that he's a better man for having done so. It makes the breed, and it gets passed on through the blood. He knows the risks he's taking so it's his business and his alone. The do-gooders are trying to squeeze the guts out of all of us. 'Yes,' they will answer, 'but the horses don't know what they're being let in for. It's cruel to them.' Nobody loves horses more than those who own them and whose job it is to look after them. As for horses not knowing, let's consider one everyone's heard of, Red Rum. It's now history that he ran brilliantly and courageously at Liverpool. It's because he feels that the fences and the field are worthy of the best he can give. When he goes to smaller meetings it's all too easy for him, so he makes a fool of himself. If Red Rum was a stallion, he'd be worth more than his weight in gold at stud. Mind you, for those that feel he should not have been cut, let me say it is unlikely that we'd have ever heard of him had this not been done. There is, of course, one other thing that has affected racing – money. It's now become an industry, fabulous prices are paid for yearlings, so I suppose it's natural that their owners don't want to put that kind of money at risk, and so are happy when things are made easier for them.

Sandown was certainly not easy, it was known at that time as 'stiff' country. This was partly because at the back side of the course there were four fences within a furlong of each other which meant that if a horse made a mistake at the first before he could get on an even keel again he was on to the second. It sorted the field out. Some fell, others if they fluffed the first three were likely to refuse at the fourth. They wouldn't jump because they knew that being a live coward was better than being a dead hero. Sometimes they'd stop so quick they'd end up in the fence or ditch, and so would their riders with them. On this particular day, although she finished nowhere, Time Enough gave Mr Usher a good ride. She was 'a safe conveyance' as he told me afterwards.

From the moment the governor gave me my first horse, life developed into a routine. I arrived at stables at six o'clock in the morning, by which time the horses would have been given their first feed by Snowy the head lad. First feed was three and a half pounds of corn, measured in a zinc bowl with a wooden handle, the sort of thing mum used for taking the water out of the copper at home on wash days. I'd start by tying my horse up, then take a skip and pick out the dungs from the litter, cleaning where the horse had staled or wherever the straw was wet. I'd put the wet litter on to an oblong piece of sacking, to be carried later to the muckhill by the four corners. On warm days there the straw would dry out and be used again for the hack. Herbert would allow no waste. While I was mucking out, Snowy would come round the box shouting, 'Your horse eaten up?' and if my reply was 'Yes, sir,' he'd continue on his rounds. If there was some feed left, I would already have worked out how much there was, such as a handful, a double handful and so on. If it was considered that he hadn't eaten properly, Snowy would take the horse's temperature and look at his teeth, so that a report could be made to the governor. Sick horses obviously weren't popular, but to the governor they were a nightmare since we might have to call the vet. Vets cost money and Herbert hated parting with it. He rarely called one. He knew horses and in nineteen cases out of twenty, he was able to put his finger on what was wrong and give them the necessary to put them right.

After mucking out, I began setting fair. This meant setting a litter of straw about two inches deep on the floor of the box, rising up at the sides to eighteen inches or two feet. At that time the straw came in sheaves held together by twisted straw. I'd undo this twist carefully, join one or two of them together and put them across the doorway. It gave the box a neat appearance. Eventually I was able to make them myself better than any farm hand. Now it was time to tend to the horse, beginning with the feet. The horse had been walking around in its box stepping on the dungs and filling up the cavities, so with a hoof pick, everything was cleaned from them straight into a skip. After exercise the same operation was performed on a wet or muddy day for the feet would be clogged with clay from the Epsom chalk, so after the picker had been used, they would have to be gone over with a sponge or a water brush. This finished, the feet were greased with a mixture of Stockholm tar and animal fat. It could be bought in five-gallon drums, but for economy's sake, we made our own. The Stockholm tar acted as a disinfectant, the fat was good for the horn of the foot and the frog. The frog is the triangular piece of the foot that has a hard sinewy tissue. It's like plastic and can be pushed in with the thumb. It is particularly important because it acts as a pump to the blood, so keeping the blood moving round the horse's body.

The dressing over of the horse began with the mane and tail, and was done with a dandy, a stiff brush. I'd take the hairs of the mane or tail in my hand and as I brushed I would gradually let a few hairs through my fingers. This motion would be continued until I could blow every hair apart. Among my tools I had a curry comb, which, when I was at home I used to clean the horse's body. I only used it once for that purpose with Smythe. Snowy saw me, kicked me up the backside and said, 'Curry combs are only used to clean the brushes in race horse stables. They're not for cleaning the horses.'

The dressing of the horse's body is done strictly to a system. I would begin with the nearside quarter, continue with the offside, lift the tail and sponge out the dock, then brush the tail back into place. I would then undo the front strap of the rug and turn it back over the quarters, so keeping the horse's kidney area warm. It was important to keep their loins and body covered, particularly in cold weather. Like every stable lad, I had to learn to become ambidextrous, otherwise it would have been as awkward as hell using my right hand on the near side of the horse. When I finished the body I would then undo the rat chain or head rope, bring the horse to the door, sponge his eyes and nose and clean out his nostrils. He was now ready to face either the day or the night, for as I said this procedure was carried out morning and evening.

After the horse had been dressed over, I would saddle him and he would be exercised for about an hour and a half. I'd be back in stables at about quarter-past nine for a cup of tea and a slice of bread and jam, then I'd start the same thing over again with the second horse. In my early days this was a hack which normally wouldn't get the same treatment as a racehorse, but because I was learning, it was probably better looked after than most of the other animals. The morning ended with sweeping the yard and cleaning the saddles and bridles so we got back to what we called dinner at around one o'clock. For most of the other lads the afternoon was free, but I had to report back for riding lessons, either using the hack or exercising a horse that had been blistered. At around quarter-past four the lads would come back for a smoke and a chat before evening stables started. This was more strenuous than the morning's work. It would be 'braces down' which meant slipping the braces from your shoulders so that they hung loose and your shoulders were free. To Herbert it also meant that you were working to your full capacity; 'Get them bloody braces down' was a cry often heard around our stables.

The evening feed was the main meal of the day. It consisted of three bowls of corn, three and a half of chaff and bran with added sliced carrot or chopped lucerne. The total weight of the feed would be somewhere in the region of seventeen pounds. That amount would be given to what we called a 'good doer'. It varied from horse to horse. It's the same as with human beings; the heavyweight boxer will sit down and eat pounds of steak, while the girl short distance runner will only want a couple of eggs on toast. The body demands the amount of food in proportion to the energy required from it. So the art of making horses lies in the art of feeding them correctly. After the feed and the same cry from Snowy of 'Your horse eaten up?', the mucking out and doing over began once again. Now while it would be nice to show how all stable lads were conscientious, this I'm afraid is not always the case. We were very human, and on occasions if we'd been working or boxing in the afternoon and feeling particularly exhausted, we'd try taking the easy way out.

To some degree, our work was measured by Snowy and the governor from the pile of 'knockers' we had on the box floor when we'd finished dressing over. 'Knockers' were the dust and dried sweat that went into the brush from the horse's body. From time to time the brush had to be cleaned with a curry comb and this was knocked onto the floor and eventually into a heap. The theory was the bigger the heap, the harder you'd been working. 'Knockers' came out white, so if you wanted an easy option you could rub your brush against the whitewashed walls, run the curry comb through it and use the whitened bits as a fake. I was of course taught this trick early on by one of the older lads. I got away with it a couple of times but I tried it once too often.

One evening Herbert came into the box. 'I see you've dressed your horse over, Philup. You've finished a bit early. Are you sure you've made a good job of it?' 'Yes, sir', I replied brightly. He then ran his forefingers up the horse's back, 'turning the coat up' as he called it. 'You sure you dressed him over?' I could sense danger, but it was too late to go back on what I'd said, so I gave him another 'Yes, sir.' He bent down, wet his fingers, put them into the knockers and then into his mouth. 'You haven't bloody well touched him, you lying little sod,' and he kicked me up the arse, sending me flying into the corner of the box. 'Now you'll start over again and I'll be back in an hour to inspect.' Well, that was that. It was no use my bellyaching, I'd been found out and even worse, I'd been caught in a lie. Still, what puzzled me was why Herbert had tasted the knockers. Later, when I told the lads, they jeered at me. 'You bloody fool, you put the wall scrapings on top of the pile. You should have mixed them with the proper knockers. The old man was licking it to see if he could taste the salt, and when he couldn't he knew you'd been pulling a fast one.'

Another thing I learned the hard way about dressing a horse was the importance of not undoing the front strap until last in case the rug slipped back with the surcingles and got round the horse's private parts. This interference can drive even the quietest animal barmy. It happened with me. The horse kicked out and reared up, ending with one of his hooves on my foot. Fortunately, from my howls some of the lads guessed something was up and were able to get me out of the box. Much to Herbert's dismay, I had to be taken to the doctor's, given a whiff of chloroform while he patched me up, and was on light duties for a couple of weeks. His mood didn't improve when he got a bill for three pounds. He held it against me forever for when he called me in for work in the afternoons and my face showed my feelings he said, 'Don't you take on about it, you owe me three quid for that whiff of chloroform you had, remember?' I must have paid him ten times over in extra duties by the day I left. While I'm on the subject of horses being driven mad, I don't know if it's common knowledge that to get animals to buck in rodeos in America, they put cinches on the horses, tight round their privates, so that they come out in the ring head down, jumping and kicking, whereas ordinarily they might well be as quiet as lambs. It's not a sport that's ever been encouraged in Britain, I'm glad to say.

Although this daily routine had a sameness about it, horses were never predictable and I learned something new every day. So I was well on the way to being a good stableman by the time I signed on as an apprentice. Though trainers naturally wanted their lads to become good jockeys and ride winners for them, their main purpose was to turn out first-class stable lads. There was a saying at the time and I think it still holds good today – 'a good stable lad is the best horse a governor has in his yard'.

3

More about learning to ride – Arse over tip in a cemetery –
Stable rats at play – Pulling the birds – Travelling lads – Drinks
on the punters – The notorious Attee Perse – Stable lads and
boxing – A 'christening' ceremony – Apprenticeship: was it
worth it? – A 'cap in hand' game – Herbert Smythe: man or
beast? – Moving stales

As I've already shown, being taught to ride by Herbert was a
rough-tongued experience. It was rough in other ways as well.
He kept a frisky pony for the first lessons. Through this animal
he would discover whether he could forget the basics and let you
ride a quiet horse out straight away. Even more important, it
would show whether you were scared, if it was going to be possible for you to conquer your fears and whether you had the guts
for the job. So you were put up and made to ride bareback while
the horse plunged around, trying every trick he knew to put
you on the ground. With my previous experience I was able to
pass that test fairly easily. It was when the pony was saddled
that as I've said, the slanging began. We had then to ride with
what was called a length of leg, for the old trainers believed
that you guided your horse with your grip and your body
weight, that by shifting your weight you could direct the horse.
It's a method that is still used in show jumping. Riders throw
their weight forward to help the horse over the obstacles, and if
you look at the old photographs of the National, you will see
how jockeys sat back over their horses' behinds with a full
length of the leg, so that they showed the bottom of their boots.

I think it was when the American Tom Sloane began riding
over here that jockeys started pulling their jerks up. Since I was
taught to ride, this has been taken to the extreme by Lester Piggott, and being the master that he is, this has enticed other

jockeys to ride the same way. The reasoning behind Piggott's style is simple – just as a man can carry heavy weights easier on his shoulders, a horse should do the same. Piggott has proved this, for by adopting this stance, he allows the horse a greater freedom of movement under the saddle. I don't suppose he worked it out like that, I've never asked him. I think it's more than likely he found he could ride better that way. He is the same as all master sportsmen, or for that matter master craftsmen. He developed his own particular style and wouldn't allow the experts to change it. In so many areas the professionals move in when someone shows promise saying, 'Oh, you mustn't do it that way' when in fact it's the natural way for him to behave and in most cases the right way. I remember the boxer, Billy Walker; when he went into the ring, slash, bang, wallop, there was no one that could stand up to him, but when he was told what his advisers thought was the right way, it was against both the style and the spirit of the man, and he went to pieces.

A trainer is there to give you the finer points for you to add to your own native ability, to bring out the best you are capable of giving. He needs patience, which is something that Herbert didn't have a lot of. He didn't believe in telling someone twice. On the other hand with horses he had the patience of Job, which was perhaps the secret of his success as a trainer. Though Herbert probably wasn't the best maker of jockeys he was able to pass on a deal of his own earlier skills for he had been a first-rate steeplechase rider, even if he did teach with such warnings as, 'You'll break your bloody neck if you do it that way.' He prepared me for the kind of treatment I later got in the army when I joined a Pack Transport company. 'Sergeant Welsh, let them bloody stirrups down, you're not bloody racing now.'

Once Herbert felt you had graduated in the saddle, he would put you out riding on Charlie. Now Charlie was the greatest schoolmaster in the world. If he thought you were behaving yourself with him he'd put up with you all day, but if he sensed he had a mug on his back, you were for it. He would make for a hawthorn hedge and drag you along the side of it, so that you'd scream and jump off, or else he would set alight and do everything he knew to throw you, and when he'd succeeded, as often he did when you first rode him, he would make off home at a gallop, stop before he got into the yard, then stroll in as nonchalantly as you please. He either broke your spirit or made it.

Once you'd beaten Charlie, the old man would tell you to meet him at the top of Six Mile Hill from where he watched his string ride out. He'd get off his own hack, adjust the leathers and put you up on him, then as the string turned for home, he'd tell you to follow it with him walking by your side so that if you got into any kind of difficulty he could put his hand on the rein. Even the quietest horse can do something stupid on exercise like whipping round, shying or taking off, and it needs more experience than a kid's got to control him. I was always expecting this to happen with Herbert's hack for the way the governor barked his instructions frightened the living daylights out of me and I thought it might scare the horse. As it didn't, I suppose he was used to it. Herbert had a bee in his bonnet about gravity and balance. I've learned to thank God that he did, for whatever other faults I may have had as a rider, I've nearly always been able to stay on a horse which must have saved me many a nasty injury. Another thing I learned at this time was to watch the horse's ears. They are a sort of early warning system as to what he's likely to do. It's impossible to explain but they transmit something to you, so that automatically you're ready for the animal's next move.

It was when I had my first canter on exercise that I got a severe attack of the butterflies. I was up on the hill with the old man as the rest of the string were going down for their second canter of the morning. He turned to me and said, 'Follow them down, Philup. When they turn into the gallop, come up behind them.' I wasn't ready for it. I wasn't sure that I could control the horse. Then I thought, whatever happens I'm not going to damage anyone else – I'll leave a reasonable distance between me and the others so that if he does take off, I'll be able to stop him crashing into them. This can easily happen with an untrained rider, the horse likes company, wants to be in with the rest of the pack, so he will go like a bat out of hell to catch them, and if he's not controlled, strike into them. It's a court martial offence in any stable. In the event, I was lucky. The horse behaved himself and he didn't do any more than he was asked. Suddenly I had the great feeling of having graduated as a horseman, confidence gushed into me. Although Herbert gave me no praise, I could tell he was pleased with me. For him it was the make or break point in a lad's training. If I'd failed he was likely to have said, 'It's no good my wasting any more of my time on you' and I would have been finished.

From now on, though less experienced than they were, I was on a par with some of the other lads. Herbert kept putting me to the test on one or two of the awkward horses. Somehow I felt he was looking for one that would beat me. Eventually he found it. I was riding a jumper at exercise when he came up alongside. 'Philup, can you control that horse on a gallop?' 'Yes, sir, I think I can,' I answered. 'There's no bloody think about it, either you can or you can't.' It was a stupid question to have put to me. I'd no option but to say 'yes'. I was sent down with three other lads to do a gallop. We were going well, warming up as we went round by the Downs Hotel. Then suddenly, back went the horse's ears, he veered off to the right and on to the road. He went past the Rubbing House and like all loose horses headed for home. I was powerless, I just sat there and prayed to God that he wouldn't slip up. When we got near the yard, he slowed down a bit and I thought my prayers had been answered and that he would dive in. But his pace quickened and he continued straight on heading for Epsom Downs station. As the familiar scenery passed by me, I kept thinking of what I ought to have done, for the horse was travelling faster than my mind. I tried turning him, but I only succeeded in pulling him into the centre of Downs Road. It only needed for us to meet a bus or a car for both of us to be done for. I thought of throwing myself off, but decided that the road would murder me. I could now see the cemetery looming up on the right. It was never a place I cared for even under happier circumstances, today it looked ominous. It also meant that I had no chance of turning with a stone wall and iron railings on the side of me.

As we reached the brow of the hill, I saw someone standing in the road. I didn't recognize him at the time, but found out later that it was Bill Larkin who trained for Edgar Wallace. He was walking up to see his horses being exercised and carrying a Long Tom, the whip that huntsmen use. When he saw us coming towards him, he let out a mighty roar and cracked the Long Tom. The horse got the message, he stopped dead, his forelegs locked and he skidded along the road. Far from being happy, I thought the bugger was going to turn over. He didn't.

He recovered himself, shot off to the right straight through the cemetery gates and started galloping round. I don't know exactly what I did, I suppose I must have tried to turn him, but the horse went straight into some gravestones, turned a somersault, I went one way, he went the other, and I sparked clean out. I could only have been unconscious for a second or two. I opened my eyes and looked straight into a grave stone. It hadn't got my name on it, so I started moving my limbs to see if anything was broken or missing. I'd knocked all the breath out of myself, and when Bill Larkin came rushing up and asked if I was all right I couldn't answer. As he dragged me to my feet, he gave me a couple of thumps on the back. I got up and saw the horse looking at me, reproachful as you please, as if it had all been my fault, then he put his nose to the ground and started munching away at the grass. When Bill Larkin saw the damage, he got a bit worried. 'Come on, let's get out of here,' he said. 'Your guvner wouldn't appreciate having to pay for these stones any more than I would.' He led the horse away fast, and I followed as best I could. When we got to the gate, Bill stopped. 'Up you get Welsh, trot him up the road and take him into the yard.' 'Oh, Gawd no,' I thought. But he didn't give me time to argue, he caught hold of me and chucked me up. 'I'll try and see Herbert and tell him everything's all right,' he said as he walked off.

When I rode into the yard it was deserted. Everyone was out looking for me. May, Herbert's maid, came running. 'Where did you get to? They're all out trying to find you. The chauffeur's driven to Epsom and the guvner and the lads are searching the Downs. Where've you bin?' I gave her a rough outline of what had happened without mentioning the cemetery. 'If I were you I'd get the horse into the box and be doing it over when the old man turns up,' May said. I agreed. Fortunately Bill Larkin had met and spoken to Herbert. He hadn't told him the true story since the governor was under the impression that I'd managed to pull the horse up before he'd taken a tumble, and it was obvious that Bill had made no mention of the cemetery and the broken gravestones. After he'd examined the horse, the governor almost complemented me on my horsemanship, and took some of the blame on himself by saying that he shouldn't have put me up on him, so I came out of the incident well. There was some talk that week in Epsom about vandalism in the cemetery, but that was soon forgotten.

Gradually I was being accepted by the other lads and becoming part of the establishment. On the whole they were a good lot. The older men, – 'lad' can mean any stable man of up to seventy or over – kept themselves to themselves. They had their homes, and wives and children, but the younger ones were as high-spirited as the horses they looked after. Perhaps because of the iron discipline of their working lives they set about enjoying their freedom with zest and energy and since the main ingredients of this freedom were drink and women, it's not surprising that they were often in trouble. Again, if you give a dog a bad name he's likely to live up to it, so there were times when the 'rats' would bite and bite hard.

Our enemies were the townies, as we called the young men of Epsom who were not in the racing world. The battlefield was generally the Co-op Hall, known locally as the Bull Ring because so many fights took place there. The occasions were dance nights, the stimulation came from the Locomotive pub which was opposite the hall, and the action came when one of the lads moved in on a townie's girl or vice-versa. Although stable lads were of necessity short and light-weight, they were fit and strong, and many were first-class boxers, so generally we had the advantage. We were also used to thinking fast and knew how to keep out of trouble. We'd reckon it had been a dull evening if there'd not been at least one good scrap. On occasions, of course, things got out of hand and the police would be called in. Most lads spent at least one spell in the local nick, but the coppers were usually reasonable towards them, they'd keep them there for the night, phoning through to the trainer to tell him they'd been in trouble, were there to cool off, but would be back at work in the morning. Very few were charged, and if they were, magistrates would be lenient.

There's no doubt that the lads, in spite of their stature, had another advantage over the townies. They had to look smart when they were riding out trainers insisted on it – their appearance helped to show off their horses, so that in the evening they would strut around the town dressed up like a dog's dinner in riding boots, breeches, rollneck sweaters and caps. Most of them too had glib tongues and a line of patter which they'd got through living away from home so they were able to charm most of the local girls. Parents didn't help their daughters with their constant warnings to stay clear of us, forbidden fruit tastes sweeter, so it wasn't surprising that on Sunday mornings and most summer's evenings there'd be a bevy of girls leaning over the fence waiting until the lads were free. Herbert would shout at them and call them names, but his tongue didn't have the same effect on them as it did on us.

We had various nicknames for the regulars, I can even remember them today, but I won't list them just in case they recognize themselves. I expect most of them are respectable married women now, grandmothers maybe who wouldn't like to recall their youthful misdemeanours. The lads kept a list of those whom they considered were the likely 'runners', always willing to mark your card or keep the form book up to date for you. They also knew those that weren't trying and if a mate of theirs wasted time over one he was soon told to save his money. Basic, perhaps, but romance comes later for the lucky ones. Girls were more frightened then for two reasons, the first was the obvious one of getting into the family way and the second was in case their parents got to know. 'Cor, if my mum and dad found out, they'd murder me,' was a regular conversation stopper. It may have stopped the talking but it didn't stop anything else.

Of course the inevitable did happen, and either there was a shotgun marriage or the sudden departure of one of the lads and the arrival of a raving mum and dad on a trainer's doorstep. Many's the lad I've known who had to change stables two or three times to stay single. Michael, an Irish boy, was one who, although he got away, didn't get away with it. He had some real bad luck. He'd been to deliver a horse somewhere in Northern Ireland. He only stayed one night, but that was one too many. The girl's dad tracked him down to our stables, but somehow Mike must have got the wire for he was away before the dad arrived. He went to some stables up north, and after a few months there thought he must be in the clear. However, the girl's father was a stayer and he and the police eventually tracked Mike down. He was arrested and packed off to Northern Ireland where he was given three months in a labour camp felling trees and ordered to pay alimony for life. When I told our lads the story they weren't sympathetic. 'Bloody fool, shouldn't have told the girl his real name.' They were right, it was never done as I found out when, as an apprentice, I started taking horses around the various meetings.

Travelling was one of our occasional perks. It meant a night or two out in a different town and getting to know lads from other stables, often exchanging information and being able to back a likely winner. It meant a few free drinks as well, for every bar had its punters and a local meeting attracted more, and since we were only there for a short time, it didn't hurt us to scatter a few tips around. If the boys did pick up a few girls, they wouldn't let on they were just stable lads, they'd choose a jockey's name out of the air and stick to it for the evening. It could have its comic moments if the girls went to the stables asking to see the jockey concerned, and were confronted by complete strangers. I often wondered how many solicitors' letters jockeys got if ever things went wrong.

In those days many of the race courses had dormitories for the lads, but it was difficult to get any sleep. Some lads would be noisily boasting into the early hours about their conquests, others would be playing cards right through till dawn. I'm still astonished at how high the stakes were and the amounts that changed hands. I've seen lads lose fifty pounds, go skint and think nothing of it. It was the same when they backed horses. They'd bring an animal that they'd got ready to win a particular race to a meeting, put half a hundred on it, and if it lost shrug their shoulders and say, 'Well, that's racing for yer.' Unlike many punters I've known, they didn't try to cast the blame, they took it themselves, it was their judgement that had been at fault.

While I'm on the subject of girls, there were certain meetings that had stars by them. Nottingham with its lace girls was a particular favourite, so was Leicester, a shoe town, and Haydock Park, a bus ride from Wigan with its mill lasses. Older married lads whose horses were running at these meetings and who preferred to stay at home or whose wives knew something of the folklore of racing themselves would often put the trip up to auction and the younger boys would pay as much as a pound a time to take their place. It was worth it to them. Take Nottingham for example, where there was a pub called the Dog and Pheasant. As you went in, there'd be the ladies of easy virtue sitting around, you'd go up to the counter with your mate and in two shakes of a dog's tail, you'd be joined by a couple of tarts with their 'You boys going to buy us a drink?' and you were in for the evening.

But the girls weren't the only attraction.

Midland and northern men were great characters who loved horses. You'd see them whispering together when they caught sight of you, they'd come up to the bar as you were ordering, 'All right Charlie, I'll see to these,' then it was, 'You lads up for the races?' and you'd be treated like long-lost friends for the rest of the evening. And as likely as not slipped a quid at the end of it for information you'd given which might or might not be of any use. Then there was the theatres and music halls. I remember sitting in the two bob seats feeling like Lord Lonsdale himself and afterwards feasting on fish, chips, or black pudding and peas.

Arthur Birch, or A. Birch as he appeared on the race card, was one of the best stablemen I ever worked with. He was also the greatest con man. He didn't do it to make a living, but to impress people and to win his drinks. He'd been a fair jockey in his time but had never made the grade, although he'd earned a deal of money, which he'd lost. He was a proud man, better dressed than most trainers, but generally without a pound in his pocket. He'd never borrow money though he'd take it of people in kind and the way he did it was an education in itself. He'd talk about his racing experiences, drop in a great horse here or a great owner there but would somehow break off towards the end of the story as if to say, 'Well, the rests racing history isn't it, and I helped to make it.' He could carry a dozen people with him sitting round a table and spinning every kind of a yarn, and the bait he used to capture his audience was a silver Hunter watch. It hung on a chain draped across his waist-coat. He'd be standing at the bar, his pint getting a bit low then take out his watch with a flourish. 'Gawd,' he'd remark loudly 'is that the time?'. Whoever he was standing next to would look round and that was Arthur's cue for action. 'I bet you've never seen a watch like that before have you?' Then he'd turn it over, press a spring in the back and it would come open. 'Have to wind it with this little key,' he'd say pointing at one hanging from his waiscoat. 'A present from a grateful owner,' he'd say and point at the engraving 'A. Birch, in memory of a great National won on Moifaa in 1904'. That sparked things off. 'Cor, you won the National? You're A. Birch?' 'Yes, that's me name isn't it, Philip?' It was easy for me to agree to that. The bloke would then call over to one of his mates

50

'Hey, Charlie, there's someone over here that'll interest you', and so the build-up to the evening began. In fact, the watch had been given to Arthur's dad, a successful jockey, and of course Arthur had heard the story of the race so often he could take his audience over every inch of Aintree. It was easy to get over the age difference because there weren't any television sets and people's memories were short. It was by travelling with horses that I got to know something about the conditions of lads who were with other trainers. I thought we had it fairly hard, but things were cushy for us compared with most of the northern stables. I could understand the weather conditions were worse there but living and money opportunities were also terrible if the lads were to be believed. I'd ask them why they stuck it, 'It's that or the dole queue,' was always the answer. Some lads came south to seek their fortune and no stable that took them on ever regretted it.

Strangely, the worst conditions I heard about and later witnessed were in the south-west, at Chattis Hill, Stockbridge where Attee Perse trained. There's no arguing about his ability to train, his record speaks for itself. It was the way he treated his lads. He had nothing but boys, twenty of them at a time, and he used them as cheap labour. They'd go to him expecting to be apprentices, raw ignorant lads they were. Some he'd take on who weighed over nine stone, who'd no chance of ever getting a ride let alone making a jockey. Most would only stay a year or so and then move on. He didn't care, there were plenty more where they came from. They weren't put into lodgings, but lived above the stables in a long dormitory and when they'd finished work for the day they were locked up inside. The head lad would wake them in the morning with three cracks from his Long Tom, anyone still in bed after that got the fourth across his body. Breakfast was a mad scramble. It was either bread and dripping or cold belly of pork with a mug of tea. Those who got to it early would slip an extra slice under their sweater so there was nothing for the slower lads. The head lad was as hard as his governor and chased the kids all the time. We had a boy come to us with a gash down the side of his head where he'd been hit with a feeding bowl, it nearly severed his ear. There's still a story going around stables of the time when Attee Perse took two men from the local pub to court for trying to get information from a couple of his lads and when a trainer goes to that length there must surely be something wrong with him.

He and I had one brush. He'd two horses that he was training for Mr Sainsbury, a member of the family of grocers and food merchants. One was William of Valance and the other Battle Zone. Mr Sainsbury for reasons I didn't know decided to change trainers and another lad and I went down to collect them for Herbert Smythe. No trainer likes to be relieved of horses, particularly one as good as William of Valance, who later won the City and Suburban, but Attee Perse was vicious to us. 'You two buggers come down to collect Sainsbury's horses? Well do it, get them out of my yard as fast as you can. Don't stand there gawping, move.' So we moved, the shortest way across the yard, which was over a bit of lawn. He screamed at us like a sergeant major 'Get orf my bloody grass, go back the way you came and on to the gravel.' As my mate later remarked, 'Cor he's one of the nicest fellows you'd never want to meet!'

Like apprentices in most of the stables at that time, I had to undergo an initiation, which it was said qualified me to learn the finer points of horses and horsemanship. It took the form of a christening. All lads had nicknames, which is why when you hear the names of horses being read by TV commentators, some of the names of the riders don't correspond with those on the board. For reasons which were obvious at the time, I'd been nicknamed Titch, so it was decided that was the name by which I should be christened. There were four godfathers, two to hold the arms and two the legs. At a given signal from the head lad, they advanced on the victim, for that's what he now was, and laid him on bales of straw while removing his clothes. Snowy then came forward, grease pot in hand and smeared the contents liberally over the private parts. This was when the rest of the lads went into action. Taking handfuls of chaff, they threw them on to the grease, all the time shouting the victim's nickname. Eventually the proceedings were closed by Snowy, and a bucket of water and a towel were handed to the victim so that he could clean himself up. I was lucky because before it happened to me, Manch told me how to play it. 'Don't just relax and let it happen,' he said. 'The lads want some fun out of it, so struggle a bit, scream and swear, and they'll let you off light. If you just lie there, they'll go on til they make you holler. It's like the girls they take on to Epsom downs.

They don't like them to rape too easy.' I found it impossible to remove all the evidence and I was a bit scared as to what Auntie would say when bath night came. She didn't turn a hair. 'See you've been christened Phil. Just as well it's over. I shan't have it to look forward to now.'

It was also early on with Smythe that I was asked by one of the senior lads if I could box. I told him I didn't know, I hadn't tried. 'Well now's your chance to learn,' he said, and he slung a pair of gloves at me. I was called Titch because I was the smallest lad in the stables, and my opponent was a good stone heavier than I was, as well as being experienced in the noble art so I didn't stand a chance from the start. In fact he gave me a bloody good thrashing. Apparently though I'd stood up to him and I earned the title of being a 'game 'un'. This gave me the incentive to prove myself, so I watched and learned. There was a club for lads in Epsom and boxing was one of the sports it encouraged, so gradually the finer points were hammered into me. Up at the stables I was always matched against the same opponent, and though I continued to suffer severely at his hands, I could sense that gradually I was getting the measure of him. It wasn't just that my boxing was improving, something happened inside me. I got the will to win, to go just that bit further. It's what they call the killer instinct I suppose, though I had no wish to murder my opponent. So the day eventually came when I found I dictated the way the fight was going and for the first time matey took a nasty punishment. But outside of the ring, he and I were good friends.

As I improved, I boxed for the Epsom lads club and later during the big meetings at Marlborough, Newmarket and Brighton. At the Dome in Brighton stable lads would fight in the interval between the big professional bouts. The two sports, racing and boxing, seemed to appeal to the same people, so all the racing fraternity would be there, owners, trainers, punters and of course the bookies. The bookies were probably the most generous; some of them may have had a reputation for meanness when paying out after a race, but it had to be remembered that it was everyone's ambition to beat the bookie. Off the course I've always found them the most generous people. If any jockey had a serious accident or was in trouble, they were the first to subscribe.

They enjoyed watching stable lads boxing and were prepared

to pay for it by putting up the cups and prizes, and by seeing the lads all right in other ways. Herbert, of course, was chuffed and didn't mind showing it when I was boxing. He'd been very useful himself in his day and of course I fought under his colours and with his inscription H.S. on my vest, so if there was any glory going he shared in it.

I had to be sixteen before I was able to sign my indentures as an apprentice, though I'd been doing the job for two years. So around the time of my sixteenth birthday I tried dropping hints to Snowy, Mrs Smythe and May in the hope that they'd pass them on to Herbert. If they did, he showed no signs of being aware of the date. Then one morning at exercise, early in the week, he rode up alongsides and said, 'You'd better tell your dad to come down on Sunday to sign your indentures and you'd better be there yourself looking as decent as you know how.' That same night after stables I caught a train home, for we weren't on the phone in those days, and gave them the glad tidings. Auntie had told me to tell dad that she would like a few words with him before he saw Herbert, so he was on her doorstep at ten o'clock on the Sunday morning, smartly dressed and carrying a couple of parcels. The one he handed to Auntie contained two of the biggest haddocks even I'd ever seen, 'Present for you ma, I smoked them meself and I've two more like it for his highness. Now I understand you want a word with me.' If he'd given her the crown jewels, Auntie couldn't have been more pleased.

After saying her thankyous she went all serious. 'Now I'm not wanting to speak out of turn about Herbert Smythe, he's a fair man and a good trainer but if he can pull a fast one over you, it gives him more pleasure than a bunch of Sundays. Now these are the terms that should be included in the indentures, the things that is that he's bound to provide. I've had some experience of him and he'll try and wriggle out of as many of them as he can, so you be ready for him.' Then she handed dad a list. 'Get them into your head before you go in, Mr Welsh, and don't let him see it or he'll recognise my writing.' Dad threw his head back and roared with laughter. 'You're my kind of woman, ma. You and me would work wonders together.' Then he walked over to her, lifted her in the air and gave her a slapping kiss on the cheek. On our way to Herbert's house dad studied the paper carefully, then

54

lit it with a match and burnt it.

Dad was still chuckling to himself when we were ushered into the Smythes' drawing-room where the two witnesses were sitting, Bill Larkin the trainer and Frank Chamberlain the vet, both drinking pals of Herbert's. Bill Larkin had helped me with my horse in the cemetery; Frank Chamberlain was one of Epsom's great vets – great, he was enormous, must have been every ounce of twenty-five stone. He was another of the old-timers, an outsize James Herriot, tweed-suited, rimless spectacles, old mackintosh and a vintage car. It was a miracle the vehicle could carry his weight. He was good with all animals but a wizard with horses. I've seen him castrate a colt without spilling a drop of blood. After dad had handed over the haddocks, Herbert poured out a scotch as if it was going out of fashion. As dad told me later, 'I knew what the cunning old bugger was doing.' They all sat around drinking with Bill and Frank both telling dad how lucky I was to be with such a fine trainer.

Eventually Herbert started going through the indentures. When he'd finished reading, dad interrupted him quietly, 'Who provides my lad's clothing? I thought that was your responsibility. Am I wrong gents?' he appealed to the other two witnesses. Herbert blustered, 'Well, I didn't think you'd mind buying the boy a suit now and again.' Dad was all sweetness and light. 'Course I don't mind, it's just that we want things to be right and proper, by the book you might say.' Again he looked at Bill and Frank. Eventually after a few such queries from dad, they both burst out laughing. 'Seems you've met your match this time, Herbert.' Give the governor his due, he took it with a good grace and once everything was settled we all signed. I took this as my cue and made myself scarce. It was the last I saw of dad that day. It must have been one of the last things he remembered doing because when mum and he came down a couple of weeks later, she was still going on about it. 'Reckon he must have spent about three hours going backwards and forwards in the train; he didn't get back home til seven. Stewed as a prune he was.' Herbert himself was a bit under the weather the next day; when he saw me, he thrust two fingers in the palm of his left hand. 'I've got you there now, Philup, right there in the palm of me hand. This is where your trouble starts.' Then he made off with an evil kind of chuckle.

He was right in one way. He had by signing the indentures taken over almost full responsibility for me. He was to be my father for the next five years. He now had the legal right to order me around and if I did anything wrong or against his wishes he could punish me. In fact his attitude didn't change and he never gave me a hiding, just the odd kick up the arse or a clout over the head. But I now fell in for extra work. I had to do household duties. I shared these with Manch Taylor, one week on one week off. It began by my collecting the ashes from the fires. These were sifted in the yard with a riddle to keep the path that ran from the paddock to the yard. I chopped wood, cleaned the boots and shoes of the house, these included May's and the three boys'. Since the three sons were now working in the yard, I used to watch them. 'Mind that bloody puddle,' I'd shout. 'Remember who has to clean your boots.' Now it was compulsory for me to go back in the afternoon to help with the cleaning of the kitchen, to pluck chickens or pheasants, draw rabbits and hares, clean out the fowl pens and collect the eggs.

When I was finished in the house, we went up to the gallops on the Downs stone picking. We had to remove the stones and pieces of chalk that might hurt a horse's foot or that he might throw up and so damage a lad's face. It was backbreaking work going up that mile and a half. Not so bad in the summer with the sun on your back, but almost unbearable in the winter with the icy cold winds biting into you. It was in the winter when we thought the stones must grow there, for we'd spend three days on Six Mile Hill clearing away tons, yet when we went back there a week later, it was as if we'd never picked one.

Stanley Wootten superintended this operation and whereas other trainers might provide three apprentices at a time, he had his whole stable staff out there as an example. It didn't matter how many winners a lad might be riding for him, he was treated the same way as the others. Stanley used his lads as whipping boys for any slacking on our part, which made for a bit of bad feeling. They'd be continually on to us to work harder so that they kept out of trouble. He'd sometimes leave us alone for a while and we'd use part of the time to have a rest, but he was cunning and would appear from where you least expected him. Then he'd start swinging his Long Tom, he was a master with it. I never saw him hit a lad, but he could crack it within half an inch of anyone's body. Once I saw him use it as they did in the cowboy films. He rode up behind his string of horses as it was returning home and he noticed one of his lads with his feet out of the irons, riding slack and puffing away at a cigarette. He got closer to him, then whipped his Long Tom round the boy's arms and body, pulling him out of the saddle and on to the ground. The kid never knew what hit him. He lay there frightened out of his wits as the governor lashed into him with his tongue. It must have been enough to put him off smoking for the rest of his life.

One other job that I now came in for was to look after any sick horse during the night. A paid lad, that was someone who'd done his apprenticeship, was not expected to work after seven in the evening, so if a horse got colic or the like, it was my job as an apprentice to sit all night in a corner of the box, a rug around me, and with the horse looking at me as much to say, 'What the hell are you there for?', and me thinking, 'For Christ sake get better and don't cause me any trouble.' So now for the honour of being able to call myself an apprentice: I doubled my money, five bob instead of half-a-crown a week, had to work all hours and at anything the governor put me to and I couldn't call my soul my own.

Herbert Smythe was a man of his time. By that I mean he was typical of many in the racing scene of forty or fifty years ago. He practised what had been practised on him. It's unfair to judge him by today's standards. I accepted and understood him, and for most of his ways I admired him, but I felt no affection for him, nor did I feel obliged to him. In many ways he was similar to my dad. They'd both come up the hard way, waiting for the main chance, always looking after number one and never relying on anyone for anything. It made them insensitive and rock hard in their attitude towards their work and workers, but outside work, to their family and friends, they were generous, not just with their money but with their time.

Racing has always been way behind the times, though recently, mostly through outside interference, too much has been tried too quickly. It's still a cap in hand game, though, know your place, touch your forelock. The discipline is strict, the seniority and rank clearly marked – Jockey Club – stewards – owners – trainers – jockeys – apprentices and stable lads. Today perhaps there are more chiefs than Indians, but before the war there was no shortage of the rank and file. Every Saturday and

Sunday fathers and their young boys knocked at every trainer's door in Epsom trying the get their lads into a stable. We knew that there were plenty more where we came from and so did the trainers. I think the best example I can give of distinctions in racing can be seen regularly at the starting gate. The starter may be a retired Army major; when calling the horses in at the starting gate, he will shout 'Get a move on Piggott, don't hang about, get that horse in.' In what other walk of life would you hear a paid official speaking in those terms and tone to a multi-millionaire and a genius in his profession? It's barrack square stuff and makes you wonder whose cap is in whose hand.

Herbert Smythe was strong, around five-foot-three tall, thick-set and weathered. He wore well-cut country-style clothes, as it were, dressing the part he played. He was very much a family man. Mrs Smythe could do what she liked with him, but she never interfered in the running of the stables. She was quiet-spoken, dignified and commanded respect. She knew a deal more than her manner gave her credit for. She understood that Herbert found it almost impossible ever to give praise or thanks for that extra bit of effort the lads put into their work, so she found the time to do it for him. 'Mr Smythe tells me you rode an excellent gallop this morning, Philip.' It meant much to us, though it would have meant more if it had come from the governor himself. She raised four sons, all of whom have been a credit to them both. They were never spoiled, as I've said, when they went into stables, they were treated as hard if not harder than the rest of us. They were, of course, given priority with rides, but no one considered this unfair and no animosity was shown towards them. Above all, they never spoke out of turn. None of our mistakes or misdemeanours, and there were plenty of them, were reported back. I thought then, and I still do now, that it's a pity Herbert didn't have a daughter, she would have taught him a thing or two while she was growing up and we might have seen something of that 'soft inside' that mum had credited him with.

There was another member of the family, May, the maid, or perhaps I should call her the housekeeper. She wasn't related, of course, but what she said went, she ruled. The governor was scared stiff of her, Mrs Smythe relied on her completely, and to the boys she was every kind of friend and relation rolled into one. She never took advantage of the power she must have known was hers. She kept her place, which I think gave her more authority over everybody. She could be a real villain to us lads, but once I got the measure of her, knew what she expected from me, and gave my services willingly, I was in, and was shown the same kind of treatment in return. She was a very useful barometer. If I wanted something from Herbert, I would ask her what the weather was like in his direction. 'A bit stormy this morning, Phil. Come back after dinner and I'll tell you how he is then.' Sometimes she'd say, 'Leave it with me, it's something I can sort out for yer.' May stayed with Mrs Smythe after Herbert's death in 1954, and when later their mother died, the boys saw to it that May was given a home and looked after until the end.

Herbert enjoyed playing his little tricks on us, although sometimes it was difficult to see the funny side. It was his responsibility for kitting us out. He was pretty fair over this, since the appearance of his lads reflected on him, so I didn't expect any difficulties when I went to him one day for a pair of new breeches. I was ready for his 'Let's have a look at the old'uns first', I'd taken them with me and I showed them to him. They were of cavalry twill, which although it didn't wear out, eventually cracked where the creases came. He grunted when he saw them, then his face lit up, 'I've a pair of me own upstairs that will fit you a treat.' Well, I was a bit dubious at first, then I thought how he would have only had the best when he was riding, so I felt there would be no harm in trying them on. 'Nell,' he called to his wife, 'fetch that pair of riding breeches of mine. I think they'll be all right for Philup.' Then he turned to me, 'Well, what're you standing there for, get your bloody trousers orf.' I was a bit shy, I didn't want Mrs Smythe to come into the sitting-room and see me standing there in my underpants, but I had no option. He didn't make matters any better, for just as she came in, he said, 'Not a very pretty sight, is he, Nell?' I stood there blushing to the roots of my hair. 'Leave the boy be, Herbert,' she said sharply and then handed the breeches to me with 'Take no notice of him, Philip.' I put them on, and as I was doing them up, Herbert called me over, pulled them up at the back and held me there. 'What do they feel like?' he asked. Well they fitted me a treat and I said so. The cloth was beautiful and I'd seen by the label that they had been made by Mr Lodge, one of the finest breeches-makers that had ever been in the business. He was used by all the leading jockeys of the time. 'Well, they're yours, me lad. They're a sight better than you'd have got at Harvey's.' That was our local firm. 'So from now on, make sure you're worthy of them.' Then he started roaring with laughter. I saw Mrs Smythe smiling too, but I thought it was at the pleasure I was showing.

When I'd finished thanking him, I took them home over my arm. Aunty, of course, noticed them straight away. 'What've you got there?' she asked. I showed them to her. 'They're a luvvly pair, but they're much too big for you.' 'No, they fit fine. I tried them on at the guvner's.' 'That's as maybe,' she said, 'but you'll find I'm right. Go upstairs and let's see.' Well, up I went full of the joys of spring to prove her wrong, but she wasn't. There was a good three inches to spare round the waist. 'Now show me where and how you were standing when you tried them on at Herbert's' Aunty said. I went through the motions and she grabbed a handful of the cloth at the waist. 'That's what the old sod was doing, wasn't it?' I agreed that it must have been, though I hadn't felt anything. 'Take 'em back straight away, silly old fool wasting everybody's time. Tell him I'll speak to him in the morning.' Back I trooped feeling no end of a narner. 'What's up, Philup,' said the governor all smiles. When I told him he roared with laughter. 'You must have lorst weight, running all that way home with 'em. Nell, poor old Philup's breeches have grown too big for him,' and again he howled with laughter. 'Never mind lad, get yourself down to Harvey's tomorrow, they'll fix you up.' I think Aunty must have had words with him because when I went to Harvey's, they'd had instructions to fit me with the very best.

Herbert liked to save money. We had a contract with a local man who collected the horse dung regularly, but Herbert found it difficult to refuse spot cash, so when a fly boy came down from town and offered him the ready for a cartload, he took it. A few days later the contract chap came round, he looked at the small heap and said, 'What's the mater 'erbert, your horses constipated or something?.' There was a stable backing on to ours, so the governor told him not to worry but to fill up from next door. I told him he was chancing his luck, that the trainer would catch on, but he wouldn't have it. 'He's off racing today, you'll find it'll be all right.' Just as our muck man had finished loading, by chance the muck man our neighbour was contracted to happened to be passing. He drove into the yard. 'What the 'ell do you think you're doing?' he said to our bloke. It ended up with the dung having to be offloaded, and the next day Herbert had to face the unpleasant music, and was without a friendly neighbour for a number of weeks. It didn't worry him, nor did it stop his thieving ways. It was his habit when we were short of lucerne to send one or two of the lads into a nearby field with sacks to pick enough for the horses' next feed. It couldn't have been more than a couple of weeks after the muck heap incident that they got caught by the farmer. Again there was hell to pay. It was just as well the lads were loyal and didn't say that Herbert had sent them. Mind you he banked on it, because when the farmer called, he put the blame their way. It didn't do them any harm, they knew they had Herbert over a barrel and were able to see themselves all right for a week or so.

The trouble with the governor was that he wasn't predictable. The day before a Lingfield meeting, Stanley Wootten offered me a ride on one of his two-year-olds, and I accepted. I knew Herbert was taking one of ours there to be ridden by his son, so the day before the meeting, I asked Ted if he'd ask his dad if I could drive over in the car with them. I was certain Herbert wouldn't mind because by getting the ride he took two thirds of my fee, and half the presents I might get from the owner, under the terms of my apprenticeship. After dinner that day I met Ted again, and he told me that he'd spoken to his dad that everything was O.K., and that I had to be outside the house at eleven the following morning.

When I arrived there, Herbert came out. 'What the 'ell are you doing 'ere, all dressed up?' he asked. I explained that Ted had told me to be there at that time. 'So you expect me to drive you to Lingfield.' I told him that that was what had been agreed. 'You know, Philup, I don't buy cars to run you around the bloody countryside,' he'd just got a new Talbot. 'Well what am I going to do?' I replied. I was now anxious. 'How much would it cost to go by coach?' he asked. 'About three and a tanner I think, but I've missed it now.' 'Well,' he said 'that's the amount I want before you get into this car.' I couldn't believe my ears. 'I haven't got it,' and it was true. 'Never mind, I'll dock it out of your next pay packet. Come on, get in.' He didn't speak to me again until we got out of the car at Lingfield. 'Well, Philup,' he asked all friendly like 'What do you think of her?' 'A very nice vehicle,' I replied. 'Hmm, that's just as well since you've now subscribed three and a tanner towards her. See you after the last race.' The old bugger was as good as his word and I only collected eighteen pence the following Friday.

Yet the same Herbert Smythe could be as kind and generous as you like to the men, women and children of Langley Vale. He was popular all the year round, but at Christmas he was Santa Claus, every kid had a present from him and he distributed food parcels galore. He held a gala night at the Derby Arms, when the drinks were on him. It was just that his business and social life were two different things. 'Grind 'em down and keep 'em there' was his motto for those who worked for him, not because he was cruel, but because that way he got results. It was how he had been treated, and the saying 'It didn't do me any harm' was very much the attitude of both employers and parents at that time.

I think I was responsible for the governor deciding to buy new stables. He'd got a gang of us decorating and distempering the boxes. It was at the time when the jumpers were turned out. He asked me if I'd ever used a blow-lamp. Quite honestly I was able to answer, 'No'. 'Well, now's your chance to learn,' was the inevitable reply. He first showed me how to light it and we got it going, so that it was roaring away like a lion. Then he explained how I was to use it with the scraper, and once I'd got the hang of it, I began enjoying myself. I finished one door and started on the next. I noticed that the door I'd just done was smoking a bit, but I thought that must be the usual way of things, so I continued working merrily. Suddenly there was a 'wolf!', and the door burst into flames. I stood looking at it mesmerised. Of course, just at that moment Herbert came back. 'Philup,' he shouted, 'what the 'ell you trying to do, set the place on fire?' 'No, sir,' I said, as I ran for a bucket of water, and threw it over the door. Herbert did likewise and we soon had the fire out. Then he stood and looked at me. He was wearing a big overcoat, he took it off, flung it over my back and then said, 'If you want to bloody well get rid of me, kick me out. Don't sodding burn me out.' After the excitement had died down Herbert went round having a good look at all the woodwork and corrugated iron, and came to the conclusion that as it was only being held together by paint, we'd better leave well alone and just give it another coat.

62

It was only a month or two later that he announced that we were to move stables. He'd bought the yard that had been built by the bookmaker, Mr Benson, whom older punters will remember as Dougy Stewart of 'Dougy Never Owes' fame. Sheeny Hiams, also a one-time bookmaker and father-in-law of George Duller, the famous hurdle race jockey, and one of the immortals who developed a new style of riding, bought them from him and later Sheeny gave the yard to George, who trained among others for Victor Emmanuel, the American millionaire. He won the Royal Hunt Cup for him with Totaig, and brought over the leading Yankee jockey, Bennie Rosen, to ride him. His stables were distinctive in Epsom because he was the first trainer to have his own horse box bought with Victor Emmanuel's money and painted in his colours, blue and white. It was more like a travelling caravan than a box. Herbert was able to get the yard because George Duller decided to move to Aston Tyrell in Berkshire. The governor never regretted his purchase.

Our new quarters were not far off, but were larger, brick-built and more modern, and Herbert's house was now away from the stables, and bigger. Previously he'd lived over some of the boxes, which must have made the nights noisy with the horses turning and scratching and rolling. In the day-time when he was indoors, he could hear more than he should have, and more than was good for us. The new stables were an indication of his success, both to present and future owners.

The actual move caused little trouble. About a week before, we cleaned the new boxes out and set them fair, and then on the allotted day we mucked the horses out, did them over and exercised them, then rode them back into their new homes. Each horse had already been allotted a box, carefully arranged so that between every colt and filly there was a gelding; it upset horses to have the opposite sex next to them. We repeated the formula for the second batch of horses and by dinner-time they were all safely housed. Removing Herbert's home took longer and was more strenuous. All the furniture was carried in horseboxes and at very little cost. We were regular customers of Richmond's, who hired them to us at so much a mile and since Herbert chose a day when there were no meetings, Mr Richmond was only too happy to let us have a couple. We took the partitions out of the middle and after ten journeys the move was complete; Herbert was as pleased as punch and we lads were knackered. It was as much as we could do to stay on the horses the following morning.

It's the gap of forty years and the social changes that have taken place during them that may make Herbert appear something of a villain today. It must be remembered that he was the son of a bricklayer, that he knew the meaning of poverty, and that in the years between the wars money was hard to come by, labour was cheap, and the universal motto was 'a penny saved is a penny earned'. Herbert was really little different in his thinking from any other employer and was typical of the racing world of his time, so if you want to understand racing, you have to understand the men who have made it and kept it the way it is now, the sport of kings.

3 North Cross Road, East Dulwich, SE22, in mid-20s. From left to
right, Dad, Mum, sisters May and Rose, and the author.

The author at 17 going down on
No Earthly to the start of the Steve
Donoghue Apprentices' Plate race.

General view of race meeting at Epsom, 1928, showing the open side of the course.

Derby Day at Epsom, 1928.

Captain Allison, chief Jockey Club
starter in 1930s.

Charlie Smirke on the 1958 Derby winner
Hard Ridden.

Prince Monolulu, the famous tipster, at Ascot, 1928.

Herbert Smythe, the Epsom trainer, discussing racing at a steeplechase meeting, 1937.

Tommy Weston (*left*) and Gordon Richards (*right*) at Epsom, 1928.

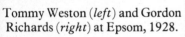

4

After I'd been apprenticed to Herbert for around nine months,
he came up to me before exercise and said, 'Philup, I want you to
ride Grand Lady Filly today.' In those days a horse could be
entered for a time under its sire's or dam's name. She was a little
two-year-old filly by the Derby winner, Call Boy, 'You do well on
her for the next four weeks and you can ride her in her first race
at the next Epsom meeting. What do you say to that?' 'Thank
you, sir' I replied. 'I should bloody well think so. I'm taking a
chance on you. See to it that you deserve it.' So, for the next
month I rode her out with Herbert watching whenever I galloped, to see if I was capable of handling her on a race course.
Grand Lady and I were two greenhorns together and though I
was chuffed at having the ride I knew that anything might
happen. I had the butterflies from the beginning and no matter
how many times I tried saying, 'What will be, will be', they
wouldn't go away. I kept hoping that they would not transfer
themselves to the horse.

It was, of course, a five-furlong handicap. I was claiming the
seven pound allowance for an apprentice. I needed it for when I
looked at the list of runners, although there were only five, I saw
that the other riders were Steve Donaghue, Gordon Richards,
Brownie Carslake and Freddie Fox, so there was I, a mug in the
company of four of the best jockeys of the day. To make matters
worse, the starter was Captain Allison, who to my mind at the

time was a bloody villain. He was the man who had reported Charlie Smirke to the stewards and had had him stood off for five years.

The great day dawned. I was up an hour earlier, as we had to be when there was an Epsom meeting in order to finish exercising before the crowds started to arrive. I gave Grand Lady a short gallop, had an early dinner, dressed in my best suit and was on Herbert's doorstep a good quarter of an hour before he came out to walk over with me to the course. Together we went into the weighing-room. Nowadays no one is allowed in except the jockeys, but then everyone was there, trainers, owners and their friends. It was a free for all, and often it would be more crowded than Tattersalls. A bloke came over to meet us, very friendly he was. 'This lad's riding for me today, George. Look after him won't you, it's his first race.' Then with a 'See you in the paddock, Philup,' he left us together. 'You're riding for my brother are you, sonny?' 'Your brother, sir?' 'Yes, didn't he tell you? I'll be valeting for you.' I had of course heard that one of Herbert's brothers was a valet but I hadn't expected to see him that day. He made me feel much more at ease, and by the time I was dressed I felt almost related.

He fixed me up with a pair of breeches and boots, and then he slung a pair of silk stockings at me. I said, 'Christ, what am I supposed to do with these?' 'You put them on, pull them up to your thighs.' He must have read my thoughts. 'It's all right, once you've got your boots and breeches on, they'll stay up on their own, you won't need a suspender belt.' I soon saw the point of them, for when I put on the boots, they slid on easily, although they were skin tight. They became almost part of me. George finally put on my colours and my cap, tucked my ears in and drew the tapes tight (jockeys didn't wear skull caps in those days). 'Come on,' he said, 'let's put you on the try scales.' These were the pre-race scales that you sat on to check that you were the correct weight, you also held your saddle, weight cloth and number cloth and there was a member of the race course staff at your side making a note of the figures in a book. 'Right, now you're O.K., sonny,' George said, and left me.

I stood there feeling a bit lonely, waiting for them to call 'Jockeys Out.' It was some time coming, so I moved over to the door, I didn't want to be left behind. At last the order came, and

I followed the four great men into the van, which took us from the weighing-room down to the course. I don't know whether George had fitted the tapes on my cap too tight, but now my eyes were going bonk, bonk, bonk as well as my stomach. I left the van and walked into the paddock ring. The governor came up to me. ''ow do you feel Philup?' 'I'm all right, sir.' I wasn't going to tell him how I really felt in case he jeered at me. 'So you should be' he answered. 'You're getting your first ride early and I'm paying you for it. It ought to be the other way around.' I don't think he meant it as harsh as it sounds. He knew I was nervous and he thought by needling me he'd rile me out of it. I knew already what my instructions were. I was giving the horse its first outing, and nothing was expected of either the horse or me, except to ride a reasonable race.

I cantered down to the starting post and Captain Allison sitting there on his hack, dressed for the part in breeches, boots, long black coat and topper. He called the roll in his deep bass voice, then moved over to me. 'Christ,' I thought, 'What the hell have I done wrong?' But he was kindness itself.

'Welsh?'

'Yes, sir.'

'You've never ridden in a race before?'

'No, sir.'

'Do you know what to do?'

'Yes, sir.'

'Is that filly good at the gate?'

'Yes, sir.'

'Good. Now take no notice of these others. You worry about yourself. When I get up on the rostrum and say "get into line", don't look at those behind you. You walk up as if you are that line. They'll follow you. Now don't forget, and good luck, Welsh.'

I couldn't have asked for more. He'd hit exactly the right note. He'd put me back on what I'd been trained to do. More encouragement was to come, for no sooner had Allison left, than Gordon Richards came up alongside. 'You ridden before, sonny?' 'No, sir.' 'Now don't you take any notice of us. Do what your guvner's told you. We'll look after ourselves.' 'Right, sir.' 'Good luck, Welsh.' My tail was right up. It seemed everyone wanted me to win. When Allison gave his command, I went up to the tapes as he'd said. They flashed and we were off. I went out front with Grand Lady going beautifully. There was nothing between me and the long greensward and the hundreds of people lining either side, with the grandstand in the distance, a sea of faces. It was intoxicating. I'd never known anything like it. Then as the two-furlong post flashed by, the feeling came over me, 'Christ, I'm winning. I'm bloody winning.' So I start pushing the filly on as we met the rising ground about one-and-a-half furlongs from the post. Then suddenly it came, whoof, whoof, whoof, whoof and four horses passed me as if I was standing still. My heart sank to my boots. I finished last.

As I rode in the governor came to meet me. He didn't look disappointed. For him he appeared almost chuffed. 'How did it go Philup?' 'It went all right for her first ride, sir.' 'Yes, I could see that, but how did you go?' 'I enjoyed it, sir.' It was the wrong thing to have said. 'Of course you bloody well did, you were making money at my expense, that's why you enjoyed it.' He took the wind right out of my sails, then he softened a bit. 'You did all right. Anyway you didn't get left, did you?' 'No, sir' I said. 'Just as well; you'd have had my boot up your arse if you had,' and with that parting shot he left me.

It was a different story in the weighing-room. George Smythe was valeting Gordon Richards as well as me, so he was changing in the same bay. 'You went very well, sonny,' the great man said. 'Thank you, sir.' 'Do you think you'll like riding?' 'It's smashing, sir.' 'Smashing it may be, but it's a bloody hard job.' I couldn't see it that way. What was hard about sitting on a horse for a few minutes and getting paid for it? I was to learn what he meant later.

After I'd changed, I went in search of mum and dad. They'd come down to watch my first ride. Despite the fact that I'd finished last, they made quite a fuss of me. Dad spoke louder than usual so that all those around would know that he had a jockey for a son. He was a bit extra pleased for he'd backed Steve Donaghue to win and he'd obliged. ''ope you didn't think me disloyal, Phil, but you did say you 'adn't got a chance.' Mum then said she'd had a few bob on me, as if that made things better. Dad had brought his usual parcels of fish, and he went down to see the governor after the meeting. The next time he saw me, he told me Herbert had seemed well pleased with the way I'd ridden, but that he'd added 'Don't tell him so, or else he might get big headed, and that's the worst sin in my book for any lad.' Trainers had strange ways of describing the qualities needed to make a jockey, 'a lad should be cocky, but not too cocky' was Stanley Wootten's way of putting it. Not too easy to work out, let alone follow, I found.

I suppose the same kind of thinking applies to horses as well as jockeys. It's no good taking the spirit out of them, but at the same time they've got to be taught to do as they're told. They have to be brought round to your way of seeing things, which is easy enough to say, but when you consider a horse has seven or eight times the strength of a man and a strong will of its own, it isn't easy to do. Some, of course, are not so difficult as others. It's when you get an awkward one that hard thinking, quick action, sheer guts, as well as infinite patience all have to combine and be brought into play. It's not a job for an apprentice, though he has something to do with it. It needs a skilled trainer who's come up the hard way, or a good head lad. We were lucky, we had both.

I've said that with humans Herbert Smythe was hard and impatient, with horses he was the opposite. He seemed to know just how much they could take, he'd sense what they were thinking, spot their faults and work days on end to correct them. He knew when wills clashed, when a horse was being purposely stubborn, and he'd search until he found a way round, but finally it had got to be his way, he had to be the master. Some of the older lads would get impatient with him and suggest short cuts, but he wouldn't listen. 'Of course I can make him do it your way, but he won't want to do it. It's our job to make him see it's the right and proper thing to do.'

He was the same with owners who wanted quick results from their horses. 'He's not ready yet. He's taking his time. We'll keep him for the end of the season, then he'll win a race or two for you', and he was almost always right. It was an education to watch and listen to him sizing up a horse. He didn't need to touch the animal, he was able to take in things at a glance. I was with him when he bid for and bought a brood mare. 'Not a class horse, Philup, but a good strong 'un.' Then as she moved away from us he said, 'Look at that, lad, she's got an arse like a Piccadilly whore. With them hips she'll drop foals easy.' He was right, and we did well with her. That remark of his stayed with me for a long time, and I found myself continually looking at women's behinds, weighing them up and assessing their childbearing capacities.

The breaking-in of a horse I found the most fascinating side of racing. You get to know your animal from the beginning, and it's like Herbert said, 'You mould the horse's character. Whatever he's like afterwards is down to you. If you don't get it right at the beginning, you'll never get it right.' You begin by putting a bridle on him and walking the horse round in a circle. You have to have a strong man on the bridle in case the horse starts lunging off. He's led first clockwise and then anticlockwise, you're simply teaching the horse to walk. He's also being guided for the first time and he's suspicious and may even be downright angry. Once he becomes accustomed to being led, you let him have more rein so that he begins walking around on his own. Again, he's not used to this so he probably stops, looks round and says 'Gawd, what am I doing here?' You may persuade him to get going again or he may try and make a bolt for it, so that you've got to get him under control and start again. When the horse can lunge from left to right and right to left voluntarily, without any problems or misbehaviour, it is time to put the roller on him. This is a piece of harness that is both a breastband and a bellyband which gives the animal the feeling of a saddle. It should not be buckled too tightly or fast, though tight enough to stop it slipping over the flanks. While this is being fitted one lad holds the horse by the bit and another by the lunge rein on the head collar. The lad on the bit is there to check the horse's head movement since some horses are inclined to rear and double up when they feel they are being restricted by the roller. When the horse is returned to his box he continues to wear the roller; it is gently removed at evening stables and kept ready for use the next day. When he's ready, you go on to the next stage.

You put a neck strap on him, the lads call it a life belt for it saves them from falls and possible serious injury. It's also used for a support band for a running martingale, which checks a horse when he throws his head in the air. Some trainers use it on yearlings. Herbert didn't. He said that if an animal was broken in properly by a good man, there was no need for him to have any other aids to riding, bar his bridle and his saddle. With the bridle and saddle and neck band, a third man comes in to the arena, who is either an apprentice or a trained lad, depending on the nature of the horse. He is put up on the horse, just leaning across him, one hand on the pommel and the other on the neck band. He pats the horse gently on the neck and talks to him, 'Wooa lad, wooa,' in a caressing sort of way. As like as not the horse's ears will go back, then forwards and he'll be thinking, 'What are they going to do? And if they do what I don't want them to do, what am I going to do?' He's weighing the lad up, as much as the lad is weighing him up. If he's lucky, the lad manages to persuade the animal that he means him no harm and eventually he slides down the shoulders and on to his feet and gives the horse a good hard pat; he may take hold of the leathers or the saddle flap and make the sort of noise with them that he would if he were getting on to the horse properly.

The next stage is for the lad to jump up again, and the trainer may say, 'I think we'll walk him on now.' It's then the lad's got to be ready because once the horse's moving, the animal really feels the weight on him and though he may take a couple of strides or so, and you think he's going lovely, suddenly, whoof, and he's off, and if the lad's been quick enough, he's baled out, and if he hasn't, he's left hanging on to the reins and being dragged along. Nine times out of ten he doesn't get hurt, and he'll have learned something. He'll have got the feel of the animal. You can tell to some extent the way the horse is taking it by the way he's moving. If he's walking in short strides as like as not he's unsure of what's happening, but if he walks with a full stride, you can allow yourself a little more confidence, lie on him longer and shift your body so that he can feel the change in weight. If he goes well like this for a couple of hundred yards, you stop, slide off, then remount with the right thigh over the top of the saddle and the left leg loose, so that you're ready to make your exit. You still keep low, so when a horse looks back he can't see anything above him. This is repeated and the horse, you hope, accepts you more each time, and you get more confident until you've done it a dozen times. By then the animal has had enough for the day and so have you. It all takes time, and time was something we had plenty of. Now it's different. Time is money and things have to be quickened up, which I think is bad.

The breaking tack is, of course, a particular type of harness, different bridle with keys on the bit, which makes the mouth lather and keeps it soft. An old trick if a yearling's mouth didn't lather was to pull around twelve strands from his tail, twist them together, thread them through the keys of the ring of the bit, anoint this with a little pure soft soap, which would produce the lather nature hadn't.

When you finally start to ride the horse, you work the bit left and right slowly. He doesn't know why you're doing it, but it teaches the horse to keep the bit level, and if it's in the middle he will go straight. If it gets lopsided, he starts hanging on the side that's protruding the most. He looks for something to lean on which is why in the form books you'll read about a horse 'hanging to the left in the final furlong'. It means he's tiring, looking for support and so is chasing the bit. It follows, therefore, that if you can teach your horse to keep the bit level it should be one fault he should never develop. Horses are like children, they'll learn something bad quicker than they'll learn something good, so it's up to you to see to it that they only know the right way to go. Once you start riding you adjust your stirrup leathers to three lengths of your leg because with the horse not knowing which way to go, you have to tell him by the use of your body weight, or by tapping him on the shoulders, always avoiding pulling on the mouth. Then later you get him alongside an old horse and let them bump and knock against each other, so that your animal gets less frightened of other horses. He's got to learn not to go berserk when he's hit in a race and the sooner he learns it the better.

As a youngster I loved riding yearlings. It taught you so much, particularly when you got a rough one. It's the nearest the jockey gets to the cowboy and rodeo style. You learn to be able to sit on a horse when it takes off with you and starts jumping and kicking. Maybe it's frightening but it's a great thrill.

No matter how hard you try with some yearlings they remain buggers. Sometimes it's to do with breeding. Nasrullah is an example; often when racing he'd go for other horses and savage them, but at his best he was brilliant. Nasrullah colts inherited his viciousness. Some horses are allowed to stay that way, particularly if they have an early success or are well bred and cost a deal of money. The owners realise that they may make a lot more when they put them to stud. More often than not though, if a colt is vicious, jumps other colts, tries to savage a lad, they've got to agree with the trainer and say, 'This is where he and his masculine parts part company', because it's the only way the vice can be taken from him. It doesn't always work, Lady Beaverbrook owns a horse called Bold Boy. Even after he was castrated, he remained a funny old devil, grabbing at a lad. They'd left him too long. It hasn't done her or Major Hearn the trainer any harm. He's a brilliant horse and has won everything in front of him. He's taken more prize money than any gelding before, but even so, they must occasionally cry their eyes out that he's not a colt, for he would have earned a fortune at stud. He's a middle-distance horse, best over around a mile and in this country middle-distance and staying horses are failing a bit, the breeding is dropping away, which is why Alleged will be such an asset if he is kept in stud in this country or in Ireland.

When Red Rum was cut he was a two-year-old, and nobody thought anything about it. He was a little horse and not well-bred, then he won the National and everyone said what a pity he's no longer endowed. But horses are no fools, and if he'd been a colt, possibly well hung, would he have wanted to tear around Aintree with the chance of catching himself on the top of fences? A horse that goes round the course doesn't want to be thinking about himself, he wants to be thinking about the job in hand, and it's no good the owners and trainers bellyaching afterwards, they're as bad as the punters who have had a tenner on a winner and moan because they didn't have a hundred on him.

Fillies were generally much easier to train than colts, but there were exceptions. I was given one to look after as a two-year-old. I don't know whether Herbert was showing confidence in me, or whether he thought I was getting a bit big for my boots and he'd present me with a bit of trouble but she was a right bitch. She was called Tetramist Filly. She was owned by a Midland bookmaker, Alf Bootle, and came to us from another stable so we'd had no hand in her earlier training. She'd been with us for about a week, when the governor offered her to me. I'd watched other lads ride her and I hadn't liked what I'd seen, and was windy of her at the start. After our first week together I managed to get to terms with her, but only just. I found myself hanging on to her three times each morning, but managed to stick there somehow. After a fortnight, we seemed to have come to an understanding. I don't know why, but she'd altered and altered a lot, so when Herbert asked me if I thought I could ride her in a gallop, I was able to say yes. 'Right,' he said. 'Now I want two of you to go down to the end of the sand track and come up as fast as you can for three furlongs. That should give us some idea of her ability.'

When I got down to the bottom of the track she started to play up, she wouldn't start, just didn't want to know. I sent the other lad back, there was no point in his hanging around, he could tell Herbert the bad tidings. Then I took the horse into the bushes, I lost my temper with her, I told her that she'd let me down when I'd most needed her, pulled out my stick and gave her a bloody good hiding. She repaid me in equal measure, she reared up, fell on top of me, broke two of my ribs and then galloped off. 'Oh Christ,' I thought as I stumbled up, 'this is one battle I've lost, it's the end of a beautiful friendship', and the pain was bloody dreadful as I made my way home. Herbert greeted me, 'You'll be glad to know the horse is back safely, Philup.' It's as well he didn't know that at that moment I was wishing her in the knacker's yard. When I didn't reply he turned to me again. 'What's the matter with you?' 'I dunno, I think I've broken me ribs.' I moaned. It didn't help. 'Gawd, costing me bloody money again. I suppose it means the doctor.' Then came the inevitable. 'You cost me three guineas once before for a whiff of gas, never got it back off you.'

I went to Doctor Heckles, until recently the doctor chosen by the Jockey Club for Epsom meetings. Herbert had obviously spoken to him on the phone, for when I got into his surgery he said, 'I hear you've bruised your ribs, Welsh. Get your things off and let's have a look.' There was no question of an X-ray. He had a feel around with me going 'ooch' every time he touched me. He wasn't impressed, he bound me up with elastoplast and with a 'you'll be all right in a couple of days or so. Don't go lifting anything,' he sent me packing. I crept back to the yard, and told Herbert that I'd been advised by the doctor to stop off for a couple of days. I thought I ought to get something out of him. 'Stop off for two days, bloody nonsense. There's bugger all wrong with you. What's a cracked rib? Nothing. It hasn't punctured your lung, otherwise you wouldn't be here.' At that moment Mrs Smythe came out. She was all sympathy. 'Herbert tells me you've cracked your ribs, Philip. You must go very carefully for a time.'

Herbert flung his hands over his face. 'Christ, women. She'd have all the lads in baby's clothes if she had her way.' In the end I did get my two days off. It was Auntie who saw to it.

I continued to ride the filly out, Herbert saw to that. 'Got your courage back, Philup?' he said. 'I never lost it.' 'All right, prove it, have another go.' He was right to challenge me. She tried everything in the book to dislodge me. She was an artist at what we call 'whipping round'. She'd be behaving quite normally, then suddenly she was gone, almost at right angles, at the same time going limp in the foreleg on the opposite side, hoping of course that I would go straight on and out of the saddle. I soon got shot of my fears and bit by bit I became the master.

I think Herbert was impressed, for one day he called me over.

'I've entered Tetramist Filly at Folkestone, do you think you can ride her?'

'Yes, sir,' I said.

'Well, I'll speak to the owner and get you the ride. Now I'm going to tell you something, Philup, she's been raced twice before and both times she's been left at the post. She's had two good jockeys on her, Charlie Smirke and Michael Beary. Now the owner doesn't give a sod how or where she finishes, but she's gotta start. He's had one or two bets with his bookmaker pals that this time she'll be away. Do you reckon you can do that?'

I'd committed myself, so there was nothing for it but to say 'yes'. Not unnaturally Tetramist Filly was very low in the handicaps, so I had to lose six pounds in weight. I had to spend the night at the Jermyn Street Turkish Baths.

I was now going steady with the local girl, Cath Allen, who was later to become my wife. She was an usherette at Epsom cinema, which wasn't a bad occupation from my point of view, as I was able to do my courting in warmth and comfort. I don't need to say that I didn't have to pay for a ticket. I arranged that I would meet her when I got back from Folkestone in our usual seats in the back row.

When I arrived at the meeting, I went up to the governor and told him I'd lost the weight as required. I was feeling a bit light-headed from doing it, and not a little apprehensive about the ride. When I got into the ring before the race, Herbert was at me again about getting the horse away, and the last words the owner

said to me were, 'Just make sure you leave that gate, and there'll
be a good drink for you at the end of it.' I got up on the animal. I
hadn't put me leg over when she started to go berserk. She
jumped the paddock rail and got stuck half one side and half the
other, with me without my legs in the irons. I kept on but quickly
abandoned ship, though keeping hold of her bridle. I think we
were lucky that she broke the paddock rail, otherwise it would
have been the devil's own job to get her out of trouble. Today, of
course, she would have been disqualified from racing, but the
stewards were more lenient then and I was allowed to lead her on
to the course and then remount her. This time she let me get my
feet into the stirrups and she was as good as gold as we cantered
to the post. The starter was my old friend Captain Allison, not so
kindly disposed towards me this time, for he'd been told what
had happened and knew something of the filly's reputation. He
gave me a lecture. 'We're not going to wait for you Welsh, and
you're not going to be given any chances. It's up to you to see
that you get away.'

I'd learned that she didn't like being out back. If she was behind other horses, she didn't want to come up to them, but if they
came to her, she'd go with them. So, when I got her to the gate, I
kept her right up to the tape, so that as the other horses moved
from behind, she'd break with them. Captain Allison must have
realised what I was doing, was kind to me and let the tapes go as
the field moved forward. The filly flew away. I couldn't believe
my luck, and as the others challenged she did not weaken. It was
the nearest I ever came to winning a race, I was beaten by a short
head. I felt bloody beautiful as I went into the enclosure, as did
Alf Bootle, for as well as the gamble he'd had on her starting,
he'd been fool enough to have an each-way bet on the horse,
which was any price, and the money he gave me for a drink
would have bought a case of champagne. I think Herbert was
satisfied with the result too.

By the time I'd got back to Epsom, and done my horse over, it
was getting late, but as I'd promised, I made my way to the
cinema to meet Cath. Things hadn't been going well for her that
evening, the manager was in a bad mood, so I hadn't a chance to
speak to her. Instead of the back seats, she bundled me upstairs,
put me in the front row of the circle, and told me to meet her outside when the film was over. My head was buzzing, so I closed my

76

eyes. The next thing I knew was that I was being roughly handled and a voice was shouting in my ear, 'What the bloody 'ell do you think you're doing?' I staggered to my feet and working on the old principle that attack is the best form of defence, I hit out, catching the night watchman, for that's who it was, straight in the belly; he doubled up with a nasty hissing noise. When I'd come to my senses, and seen who it was, I was all apologies and tried to explain what had happened. He didn't want to know. At first he was for sending for the police, and charging me with assault. Fortunately, he contented himself with dragging me down the stairs by my collar and chucking me out.

By now, of course, Cath had given up waiting. I didn't look forward to meeting her the next day and I was right not to. The night watchman must have got the gist of what I'd told him, for he'd spoken to Cath about the incident, partly blaming her for having a maniac as a boy friend. He'd also told the manager, who hadn't taken it kindly. Cath waded into me. 'You nearly got me the sack, you bloomin' idiot. I told the watchman he should've left you there, made you stew in your own juice,' and so it went on. It's been an extraordinary thing in my life, that whenever something good has happened, something bad follows hot afoot.

Not unnaturally, after a day or two back to the old routine, I was interested to know what had been decided about Tetramist Filly's future. 'Hadn't we better start thinking about a name for her?' I suggested to the governor. 'Alf Bootle's already christened her, she's "The Lakes of Kilearney,"' chuckled Herbert, and as any cockney would I laughed with him, for it's the rhyming slang for 'Barmy'. 'But it won't be necessary,' he continued, 'Because of the race she ran, we've been able to sell her. She's being shipped out to Penang in a couple of weeks time. Thank Gawd there's one born every minute, or we wouldn't be in business. We'll be well shot of her.' In a way I was disappointed, I might have had my first winner with her, for I was sure they'd never have given her to another jockey, even if they'd found one to take her on. On the other hand, I'd been lucky with her this once, who knows next time out she might have murdered me. I think that the story shows the value of a stable lad who takes pains with a horse, gets to understand it, even though it may be a villain and finally gets the best out of it. Of course, the horse has got to have something to give, but someone's got to make him give it.

There was an example of this recently, shown by a horse trained by Clive Brittain, Petronowsky is his name, and he's owned by Captain Lepos. Petronowsky was a villain, he just didn't want to know about racing, so they put him to stud and he covered about fifteen mares. He was no good at that either, his mind wasn't on the job, and his fertility rate was bad, so they brought him back to racing. He was put in the hands of an experienced trained lad, Geoff Smith, or Smudger as we all call him. I watched the horse win at Ascot in 1978 and after the race I told Smudger how much he'd improved. 'D'yer know, Phil,' he said 'When I got him he wouldn't go anywhere, wouldn't do a thing. It's been uphill work all the way, but at last I got the understanding of him and now he'll do anything for me.' Which brings it down to one thing, you've to know your animal, his character and his characteristics. It also proves what I've said before, that a governor is only as good as his staff. But now I'll add something else, and that is that a staff is only as good as its governor. He chooses and moulds them and it becomes a team effort. Petronowsky went on to win four or five other races. Smudger is the sort of lad I like. He often tries the unusual; sometimes if a horse has been awkward, instead of giving him a slap on the behind, as expected, he'll give him a pat on the neck and talk to him, sort of coaxing him to do better next time. Of course, he's strict with horses, he's got to be, but he never knocks them around. He cajoles them into his way of thinking. The stick has got to be used occasionally on gallops, but as sparingly as possible. It's often enough just to give the horse a sight of it and a stroke of it down his flank.

When it comes to racing you want a good jockey who will follow instructions. I remember once after the war, when my governor couldn't get to a meeting, I had to instruct Jimmy Lindley when he was just a kid. He listened to me as if he was hearing the Bible for the first time, it was 'yes, sir, no sir' even though I was only a travelling lad. During the race he followed what I'd told him to, just urged the animal home, no sight of the stick and won the race for us on Bowral Boy. It was only his second or third winner and he was as excited as if he'd won a big race, as of course, he did later, many of them. He was a great jockey, who if he hadn't had weight problems and the ill health that follows continual wasting, would have been even greater.

Some jockeys can be a menace by giving a horse too hard a race, some even knock spots off them when they should know they're winning easily. This means that if you have a horse who's entered again in a week or a fortnight's time, he's put back instead of improved. Any animal gains confidence if he wins easily and without punishment and will probably improve a few pounds for his next race. But if he's been hurt it sticks in his mind and may adversely affect his running, he's not thinking of the job in hand, he's thinking of the consequences.

In a way a good stable lad is a bit of a psychiatrist. Horses have their worries and their unaccountable bad habits, but if you start messing about with them, they'll very likely lick you on the face for your pains, which is all very friendly but it gets you nowhere. There are certain habits that you can do something about. One of these is weaving. You occasionally get a horse that walks into his box after exercise and starts moving from side to side instead of going to a corner and resting. They use up their energy which you hope is going to win you a few bob and wear themselves out. They also wear you out, for if you watch them for long you stagger away giddy. The way we used to cure this fault was to hang old car tyres on cords from the walls or rafters, so that when the horse went into the box, he disturbed them, and they began swinging, hitting him on his side. When that happened he stopped weaving until they stopped swaying. When he started again they began moving, and as a horse doesn't like this continual hitting, he moved into a corner and settled down.

You also get horses that walk the box, continually moving their feet up and down and threshing their straw to dust. The same procedure sometimes works with them, but not always, and unless the horse is brilliant, and you know he'll win a race for you when you want him to, the only place for him is out of the yard. Then there are horses that are crib biters and wind suckers. If you put them in a box with a manger, they'll grip hold of it with their teeth and suck the wind down their throat making an ugly sound. A bad one will also do it with anything he can get his teeth round. There's a special device to prevent this, it's a leather-on-metal collar with four prongs on springs which dig into the horse's neck as it swells before he sucks in the air.

Like human beings, horses masturbate, which wastes their strength, and though there are plenty of people around that say it's good for us, I can assure you and them it isn't good for colts. So, spoil-sports that stable lads may be, they have to stop them. There are ivory rings sold for the purpose, coming in varying sizes, declining as the horses get older, which fits in with the general run of things. A horse pleasures himself by rubbing his prick on his belly. To fit the ring, you soap your hands and wrists in warm water, put it under the sheath and over his main organ holding it between two fingers. It's easy to find where it has to fit, since there is a section which starts to get thicker. The idea is that when the horse begins to feel randy, the organ swells, the ring bites into his flesh and the pain puts him off, as it would anyone, animal or human. Once in position these rings stay put but have to be taken off once a fortnight for cleaning. I'm sorry if this paragraph offends anyone, but it's all part of a stable lad's life.

Fillies, I'm glad to say, are better behaved, they just come into season. This can occasionally be awkward if they look like coming on early and they're entered in a race, for fillies don't run well in that condition. I learned one way of putting them back a few days. It was crude but effective. I'd pick a bunch of nettles, put the filly in the paddock, have one lad on the bridle and another on the tail and at the given word, it was up with the tail, in with the nettles, down with the tail and all run like buggery. The filly would then go spare, the nettles would of course, fall away, but the stinging was enough to keep the horse mad. It was the shock of such treatment that put them off for a time. Some kinder stables would use vinegar, which would sting, but I think was less effective than the shock treatment. Again, as with human beings, there is always an exception to every rule. One filly arrived at a meeting well in season. Despite her condition it was decided she would run. The bookies, who get to know everything, were prepared to give any price about her, and were surprised when at the last minute there was a gamble on her. She walked the race. As some joker said afterwards, 'She was bloody but unbowed.' It seemed the stable had got to know that she went better in this condition than at any other time, and I think I'm right in saying that Gordon Richards rode her once or twice. It all goes to show that nothing's certain in racing.

While we were still in Herbert Smythe's old yard, we were continually plagued with rats. Regular visits by the local rat catcher helped to keep them down, but where there's corn and straw about they always come back and when you opened a box in the morning, as like as not, a couple would zoom out. There was one box though where this didn't happen. In it was a horse called Braygola, looked after by an old lad, Bill Moore. According to Bill, his horse used to kill the rats by stamping on them, and he'd bring them out in the morning and show them to us. We didn't know what to believe so we got Bill to lay on a demonstration for us. We caught a couple of rats in a cage trap and set one loose under the straw. We lost both sight and sound of it, but Braygola didn't. Back went his ears, as if he were waiting for something, then up and down went one of his forelegs and there was a 'wheep' as the life was squashed out of the rat. That started something. He was our star turn and we used to feed his box with rats. We'd try every way to fool the horse, piling the straw around him so that we thought he couldn't detect any movement or noise, but he beat us. Braygola always got his man.

Some horses are nutcases. Such a one was a three-year-old filly, Merritondy, by Glamering out of Tondalayo. She won the London Spring Handicap for us at Alexandra Palace. She wasn't a wrong'un, but she wasn't easy. She was given to walking her box. At the time, Herbert kept a goat in the yard, Gawd knows why for he was a great big bugger, like a small race horse, black, and as vicious as you would never wish a goat. One day he must have wandered into Merritondy's box. From that moment they became inseparable and she as quiet as a lamb, a different animal, and she began winning races. Now you would have thought that the goat would have protected her, but it was the other way around. At the beginning, when the lad went in to feed them, he'd put the filly's feed in her manger before pouring his into a bucket on the floor. The goat was greedy and impatient and jumped up at the manger the moment the lad began filling it, trying to get in first. Naturally the lad clouted it off. Merritondy wasn't having her mate ill treated, so she bit him in the arm. From then on it was goat first, horse second.

We were short of horses around then, so the governor put us on painting the boxes. The sun must have been shining out of my arse at the time, because when he gave me my pay packet he said, 'There's an extra quid this week for the painting you've done, but don't tell any of the others or they'll all be around demanding something.'

Had he known what was to follow, I don't think he'd have been so generous. One evening a mate and I were working late, it was getting dark, so we cleaned up in a bit of a hurry and instead of putting the brushes in turps, we laid them on the box floor. The next morning we did our normal stable work, and while we were riding out, the goat must have wandered into the box, and chewed away at the brushes for when we went to do our painting in the afternoon, they were eaten down to the handle. We got some more brushes from the governor, pretending it was our hard work that had worn the bristles down and set to again. The following morning we arrived at stables to find there was all hell to pay. Merritondy was going potty and the goat was lying dead in the litter. We didn't let on what we knew must have happened, that he'd died of lead poisoning, and Herbert didn't ask for a post mortem, so no one was any the wiser. The governor bought another goat, but Merritondy didn't take to it, led it a hell of a life and was back to her naughty tricks again. Herbert accepted the inevitable and sold her while the memory of her achievements was still fresh. He got a good price for her, but I don't believe she ever won a race again.

The real nightmare for anyone who cares for horses is when an animal gets cast; it can happen wherever he is. It generally occurs at night when he's settling down. He scratches around, gets his litter into a heap, rather like a dog making a bed for himself, flops down in it, rolls over on his side and back again, wriggling around in the straw, then he gets up, shakes himself, feels satisfied, and is ready for his rest. Occasionally you get one who doesn't gauge it right, he rolls over and ends up on his back, his side against the wall, and his legs in the air. He finds they're too far over to be able to swing his weight back, he hasn't room, he's stuck. He's like a tortoise on his back, so he panics. He's not the same as a donkey or a mule, who'll wait till eternity for someone to come and help him. He starts going crazy, and the more he struggles, the worse state he gets into, and he ends up on his side, with his legs screwed up, unable to move. And with all this mad effort, he may twist a gut, and if he doesn't die before he's found, he'll have to be destroyed. The reason for this is that a horse's gut starts at his mouth, twists around and comes out the other end. This is what makes them compulsive eaters. They can put their heads down and eat and eat, and as their stomachs fill, it goes round the gut, they dung and this makes more room for eating. So if they get cast and twist a gut, their digestion ceases to work and they're in terrible pain. It's the same as when a man gets a bad hernia, but the difference is that humans have three movements of the stomach, and two can carry on working while the third is operated on. The horse has only one, and so there is nothing for it but to reach for the gun.

It's action stations if a lad goes into a box and hollers, 'This horse is cast'. Others immediately fly over, one sits on the horses head, which takes half the strength away from him, two take his tail, and if he's lying with his legs against the wall, they pull him away by the tail. Now he has the chance to jump up. At a given word the three lads move and whip out of the box as quick as they can, for when he gets on his feet the horse jumps and kicks enough to murder anyone in his way. As soon as you can get him into the yard, where he can't do himself or anyone else more damage, he's watched to see how he's walking. If he wants to be continually on the move, it's a danger sign. Then someone puts an ear to his stomach; if it's working normally his belly rumbles away with the sound of water going through a sewer. But when his gut is twisted, there's no noise at all, complete silence. All you can hear is his breathing. Then it's curtains for him and a court of enquiry at the stables.

Unreliable horses have no permanent place in gambling stables, and both of those I worked in could be called that. To the racing stewards and the Jockey Club, gambling stables are bad news. The authorities lay down the laws, which say that any horse that starts in a race should be at peak fitness and trying to win every inch of the way, thus giving the spectator and punter a square deal. Laws, though, are there to be broken, and I'm sure the spectators and punters know that some horses are there for a ride, some because their owners want them on the course to show off, for some it's a final outing before a race their trainer wants them to win, and some run to reduce the penalty for a future handicap race. The authorities know this too, most of them being, or having been, owners themselves.

What exactly does a gambling stable mean? Let me say straightaway that it doesn't mean the stable fixes the race, this is something that is so rare today as to be almost nonexistent. It means that a horse is saved to try and win a particular race. The trainer studies the entries and withdrawals and comes to the conclusion that his horse at its peak can beat any of the opposition at their peak. He can never be certain, but he can get as near as is humanly possible. The whole business is kept secret although some fool owner may let the cat from the bag to his friends out of vanity. On the day of the race the horse, because of its past record, opens on the books at a good price. At a given moment the boys enlisted for the purpose move in on the bookies and the gamble is made. The trouble is that one or two other owners may be doing the same thing, and in the end it blows up. It does happen that some trainers come to terms with each other beforehand, and agreements are made that if one horse wins this race, he won't be trying in the next when their horses are entered together. Jockeys are rarely in on the transaction, they get their orders and may simply be told that there's so much at the end of it if they win, or that they're to give the horse an easy outing as he's being saved for a later race. Of course, accidents can happen, and they can result in a lot of angry words and bad feelings. The point of all this, apart from greed, is that it costs a lot of money to keep a horse in training, and unless it's a real good'un, it's not going to earn enough from prize money to pay its way. Bank notes are the same whether they come from a small meeting or from Ascot or Aintree.

Gambles, however, can only be brought off by reliable horses, horses that produce the form they show at home when they race on the course. You sometimes hear a trainer say after one of his has won, 'He's a funny old devil, he never shows the ability at home that he does at a meeting.' The trouble with an animal like that is that he's got too many brains. When on a race course he knows what's expected of him and he gives his best, but when he's at home, going out day after day and doing the same exercising and gallops, he thinks 'Why should I trouble to work hard? I'll save myself for when it's needed.' Such a horse is too big a risk for a gamble, so the trainer runs him in the hope of getting a bit of honour and glory and gets rid of him at a good price, which is the only way the horse can make a real contribution to the running of the stable.

Blinkers are another hazard that trainers risk. They're used much more today than they ever used to be. To my way of thinking, they should be a last resort. They transform some horses but there's many who resent them and go badly in them. Sometimes it does a horse good to run a race in blinkers, though you know he'll do badly, then to race him again quickly leaving them off. He's so surprised to find his sight unhampered that he may do well. There's the occasional horse too who is only mediocre when he runs with the field, so it's worth trying to give him his head from the start, putting him in the lead straightaway and hoping that he'll stay there and win the race.

I'd been apprenticed for about three years before I was initiated into the world of jumping. On exercise I'd had some practise with flat racing horses, taking them over small bushes or clumps of gorse, or when I was in the woods, over boughs of trees, but I hadn't had any proper training. I was beginning to put on weight. This was particularly clear because of my boxing. I'd started out at under five stone twelve, and was now up to six stone seven. I don't know whether Herbert had noticed this, but one day he put me on schooling hurdles. Once again it was two mugs together. We went down to the bottom of the paddock where small hurdles were placed against the hedge, so stopping the horses from running out on one side, and there was a lad on each hurdle on the other side who, when he saw a horse trying to veer out, would shout and wave his arms about to keep it on course. We progressed gradually. After the horse had mastered the short one, the hurdles would be placed short, medium and tall until of course finally they were all full size.

I was just about getting the hang of things when one night at a dance at the Bull Ring a lad from another stable took against me, and we stepped outside to settle our differences. He gave me one or two bruises and a black eye, but I put him out cold, and his mates had to carry him back home. Apparently he was off work next day, for his trainer got to hear about it and paid a visit to Herbert. Later May was to tell me he got small change. The governor, however, had me on the mat.

'I hear you've been disturbing the peace, Philup. Tell me what 'appened.'

'The fellow called me a ponce, sir, and I wasn't standing for it.'

The governor lost control of his face, and began chuckling.

'I don't blame you lad.' Then he stiffened again.

I don't blame you for hitting him, but I do blame you for fighting in the streets. People know you're working for me and it gets the stable a bad name. Anyway, bugger off and try not to do it again.'

The next day I was schooling a three-year-old over small hurdles. In those days they had one and a half mile hurdle races for three-year-olds. They've been stopped now; they were considered too dangerous, for with the shorter distance the jockeys would go like hell, and when a horse fell travelling fast, he often had a bad accident – so incidentally did the jockey, but I understand it was for the horse's sake they cut them out. Nowadays the distance is two miles so the pace is slower.

Herbert Smythe came down to the paddock, to watch me on so I thought. 'Philup,' he said, 'I want you to come along with me.' We went to the yard together and into one of the boxes. 'Take that sheet off,' he said and I did what I was told. The horse under it was Cherry Pie, a three-year-old gelding, owned by Merrick Good, chief racing correspondent of the *Sporting Life*. He had run over the flat during the summer and hadn't done too well, so the old man's idea was to try him over hurdles. I stood there for a second or two, feeling like a spare part. I was expecting one of the experienced schooling lads to come along and ride him. 'Well, what're you waiting for, get on the bloody thing. You set about a stable lad in Epsom High Street and knocked him around, now let's see how much guts you've really got. You're coming down with me to school this horse over proper hurdles. There'll be three other jockeys there to show you how.'

There's no denying I was scared stiff, but I hadn't any option. Even if I had I wouldn't have taken it. It was the same as in the army, I was more scared of showing fear than of the fear itself. The schooling area at Epsom was in the middle of the course. Waiting there for us were four other riders, Keith Piggott, Lester's father who was our first jockey, Bill Redman, Ron Smythe, one of Herbert's sons, and a paid lad of ours, Jack Harris.

Keith Piggott rode up to me. 'You haven't been schooling before have you, Phil? Now don't worry, keep between Bill Redman and I, and we'll look after you.' Then he gave me a few tips. I began to feel better. Bill Redman also had a word with me. He was a particular hero of mine, an Irishman with the guts of a lion. Nothing frightened him. He'd ride anything. I've seen owners and trainers going into a weighing room, looking for a jockey to ride a horse of theirs, and if any of their animals had the reputation of being a villain, most of the lads would run and hide in the lavatory. They didn't want to know. But Bill would be there, standing at the door waiting to be asked. 'Certainly guvner, course I'll ride 'im for you.' Some thought him a fool and a lunatic, for he'd broken practically every bone in his body but to my thinking courage should never be mocked, and I loved him for it.

So with the support of Keith and Bill I got through that morning's schooling in one piece and with a bit more experience under my belt. When I say I jumped perfectly, I'm not being bigheaded. They saw to it that I did by keeping their horses alongside me, so that when they went, Cherry Pie went with them. I was just a passenger, all I had to do was to sit there, look the part and go through the motions of doing everything right.

I'm glad to say that for once Herbert showed pleasure at my performance. 'You went all right, Philup, let's hope you go as well on the next outing.' I knew he was chuffed, because Mrs Smythe went out of her way to speak to me and to tell me that her husband had spoken highly of my ability.

It wasn't long after this that I was schooling over fences. Again I wasn't ready when Herbert introduced me to a big horse called Masseur, a six-year-old, originally trained by Douglas Pennant, who'd been made clerk of the course at Folkestone, and who'd handed some of his horses to us to look after. Masseur had already got the reputation in our stable of being an awkward bugger, and once again I was apprehensive as to what would happen when I took him over the training fences. On his first run, and it should be remembered that there were only two obstacles to be cleared each time, he went beautifully, but the second time his blood was warming up, and he went through the gap at the mile post, across the main course and I had visions of a non-stop ride into Epsom, when he decided he'd had enough just as we got to the road near Tattenham Corner. I expected a rollocking from the governor, but once again he seemed quite satisfield. 'You didn't get on too badly did you, Philup?' 'No sir, but I couldn't pull him up, he's a bloody hard puller.' 'Oh, you'll soon get the better of him,' he said as he walked away.

I hadn't his faith, so I went to see Snowy and he suggested that I rode him with a double bridle, which means what it says, an ordinary bridle on top of a snaffle and curb, which pulls a horse up dead. Snowy had a better idea. 'You'll get in a bloody tangle with a double, but I've got one that'll hold him,' he said. 'It's a double ring bridle, I've had it in the saddle-room for years. It'll hold him while he's in a restricted area, but it won't be needed when he's racing because he's there to go.'

The next time I went schooling with Masseur, the governor who never missed a trick said, 'What the 'ell have you got that bridle on for?' He'd have made me take it off if it had been my own idea, but I had him over a barrel. 'Snowy thinks the horse will go better in it.' 'Oh he does, does he?' It was obvious he didn't approve, but he couldn't undermine Snowy's authority, so it was allowed to stay on. From then he was a different horse and I was able to handle him easily.

We must have done well together because the day actually arrived when Herbert said, 'I've got him entered for Windsor, Philup, and I'll give you the ride.' When I saw the list of runners for the race, I wasn't as enthusiastic as I'd been when the governor had offered it to me. There were around forty entered, and well over thirty of them ran. Today they have a safety limit of runners which is governed by the length of the fences, and the number of horses that can jump in safety. But in those days if forty were entered, forty could run. Obviously this meant that the chances of a serious accident were greater because if the man in front fell, the rest would gallop over or into him and he could be kicked to kingdom come in the process.

I went to the weighing-room, and found I was in the company of some excellent jockeys. Frenchie Nicholson was there, so was Gerry Wilson, together with my old pal Bill Redman and Bruce Hobbs, who was about seventeen at the time and had yet to win the National on Battleship. I knew Frenchie Nicholson because he was serving his time with Stanley Wootten, alongside me with Herbert Smythe. He was already a good and experienced jockey. He was later to teach Pat Eddery to ride, so I'm not criticising him when I say that he was a bit windy. It's a jockey's job to assess the race, to find out where the troubles are likely to be and to do his best to keep out of them. If he's on a fancied horse he doesn't want a load of idiots or loose horses around giving him trouble. He came up to me and said, 'Phil, I don't like the look of things, it's bloody dangerous with all these horses in the race.' I was already worried because it was my first ride in a chase, now I started thinking, 'If a bloody good jockey like him is worrying, Gawd knows I should be a nervous wreck.' Then the feeling came over me. 'There's nothing you can do about it. You chose the life, you've got to do your job and take what comes.' It was the old story, I was green; the more experienced you are the more you know what can go wrong.

When 'Jockeys Out' was called, I made my way into the ring and joined Herbert, who was with the owner, the Dowager Lady Penrhyn, a game old girl of around seventy. He took me to one side. 'How you feeling, Philup?' 'Fine, sir.' 'No you're not, you bloody liar. You're windy. I can hear your teeth chattering.' He was smiling a bit as he said it. He knew what was going on in my mind, he'd been through it himself, and he spoke rough to snap me out of it. Then he introduced me to Lady Penrhyn, and ended by saying, 'This lad cost me three pounds for a whiff of chloroform when he let a horse jump on his foot.' I groaned inwardly. It was the same old story. 'I hope you've recovered Welsh, and that it won't affect your riding today,' the old lady said, all sympathy. 'It happened five years ago, Ma'm.' I replied. She turned on Herbert. 'Then what are you making all the fuss about, Mr Smythe, I think it was rather a footling remark for you to have made.' Herbert was flattened. It was the last I ever heard of my early painful experience.

When it was time to go down to the start, he tried to get his own back. 'Well, goodbye, Philup. See you in 'ospital.' 'I'll be all right,' I shouted back at him, but I wasn't so sure. When I got to the gate, Frenchie Nicholson came up to me again. 'Are you going along, Phil?' he asked, which meant was I doing my best to win, or was I just having a schooling round, running the horse for experience, which in those days was accepted, if not permitted, but which today, although it still goes on, is a court-martial offence. 'No, I don't reckon to win,' I said. 'But I won't be able to hold him back. This old bugger pulls.' 'Right,' he says. 'If you're going like that I'll stick with you. I'll tuck myself beside you.' Together we went to the gate and we were off. Now it's a funny thing about riding over fences. Once you're going, all your worries disappear. You may be in debt up to your eyebrows, your wife could have left you and your daughter be in the family way, but those things just don't matter any more. All you're concerned about is getting round that course safely. Of course you've got to win if your horse is trying, but that's only part of it, so everything you've been taught comes into play.

My main concern was letting Masseur see the fences. I didn't want him jumping too soon, either landing on one or hitting the top and turning over. It was the first fence I was most scared of. I could see it coming nearer and nearer, hear the horses galloping and the thunder of hooves behind me and Masseur was pulling away on his own, I hadn't got proper control of him. When we reached it he went sailing over like a bird, he jumped it so well that he went to the front and I was told later that when I got to the second we were six lengths clear. Again he jumped that one easily. I knew that the others would eventually catch me but I thought that if he goes on like this, every fence we get over is one nearer home. I now settled down in mind and body: I was able to think about my job as a jockey, instead of just being a passenger. Then we got to the water.

It was the first time I'd ever tackled a water jump in my life. I looked at it, a small fence only three and a half foot high but with a width of water about fifteen foot long. In taking it I must have lost my concentration, for the horse jumped it from underneath, so that instead of my going with him, he went that bit before me and I lost an iron, the stirrup coming off my right foot. This meant that I dropped to one side, and I'd only got a furlong, or at the most a furlong and a half, to get my foot back in – if I could, because sometimes stirrups can go forwards, catching in the front strap of the saddle, and they don't come back. Now the panic set in. I couldn't find the stirrup and I was getting nearer and nearer the next fence, and I knew that the least bit off the centre of gravity when I jumped it was liable to make me fall. I put my hand down in desperation. Luckily God was on my side, I found it and slipped it over my foot just before we came to the fence. It was now that Bill Redman came alongside me. I don't know whether he'd seen I was in trouble, I don't think he could've, because he began chatting to me as if we were sitting over a drink at a pub bar. 'How you going Phil? Lovely day for your first ride. Things all right with Herbert?'

I supposed I gasped something back. Then just as we approached the next fence he said, 'Stick with me lad, and you'll be all right.' I thought to myself that was the best bit of advice I'd been given that day. We took it together. Out of the corner of my eye I saw him going, the worst fall anyone could have had, with him and his horse rolling over and over. I knew he'd broken his collar bone six times, but I thought that this time he was a gonner. I was wrong. Neither he nor his horse had a thing happen to them. The rest of the race went uneventfully for me. Bill's fall didn't affect me too much, I was still too concerned for myself. I came in seventh, which was bloody good for two beginners.

Masseur won next time out at Leicester. Gerry Wilson was on him, and he skated in. I wasn't peeved that I didn't get the ride, after all I was only a kid. I'd achieved my immediate object, I'd had my first ride in a chase and I'd made everyone happy. To me life was a garden of roses.

5

Prince Monolulu – 'Gully, gully, gully!' – Jefford Brown – The professional punters – Bookies' place in the racing game – Trainers and bookies – Stopping a horse – The racing crooks – 'Ringer' Barry – Doping – 'Boidy' Davis – We win with a 'doped' horse – Deceiving the punters – Selling plates

Racing is different from any other game, with as many hangers-on getting a living from it as there are legitimate participants. I'm not complaining, they have their place, they add colour to the scene, and though at times a few of them smear it with dirty fingers, others are as fascinating as the horses and riders. One character remembered with affection was Prince Monolulu, a big man in every way, in size, personality and heart. There were many tipsters but none that could be compared with him. He was on terms with royalty, dukes and lords, as well as being the friend of the common man. It was not just his colour that attracted attention at a time when black faces were a rarity, or his feathered plumage, or the accuracy of his tips, which I suppose were no better or worse than others. He brought to any meeting a touch of pantomime and gaiety that could raise a smile even from a punter who'd gone skint. His shout of 'I've got a horse' was music in the ears of anyone approaching a course. It was the signature tune of the racing scene.

His origins are obscure, some say he came from the dockland of Denmark, but he insisted he was an Abyssinian Jew. He had travelled Europe as a young man and spoke many languages fluently. I met Monolulu early on when I was working for Herbert Smythe. Manch Taylor and I had dolled ourselves up in breeches, leggings, sweaters and caps for Epsom Sunday, and were strolling the Downs hoping to be taken as jockeys, and in that way to pull in the girls. As we got near the Downs Hotel, later rechristened the Rubbing House when the brewers discovered it was a stage post for Londoners going to Epsom races, we heard that cry which was to become so familiar to us, 'I've got a horse.' We made our way towards it, and elbowed into the front of the crowd that had gathered around Monolulu. He began spieling about his sources of information, when suddenly seeing Manch and me, he seized us by the arms and dragged us either side of him. 'It's jockeys like these two here that tell me what I want to know and what you want to know. Isn't that right lads?' Since he was playing the game our way, we agreed with him, and stood there answering yes and no to his questions until he'd finished his spouting. Then he sold his tips. They went like hot cakes.

'Stay there lads, I may be needing you,' he said as he wandered around the crowd. When there were only a few stragglers left, he came up to us, handed us a card and in a loud voice shouted, 'There you are, one of them's the tip you gave me, the others are certainties as well, and I'm going to give you the money to back 'em with,' and he slipped us half a dollar each, the equivalent to a week's wages. 'See you later boys,' he said, then he bellowed out his cries again, to collect another crowd. As we walked away some of the fly boys followed us. 'Let's see your card and we'll give you a tanner.' It was no skin off our nose, so we handed them over. They were no help, they just showed a number for each race. 'Here, what does this mean?' they asked. 'They're the numbers of the horse that he thinks will win the race. You'll find 'em on the race card or in the papers.' This set them back, they'd expected to find a name, but the Prince was a wily old bugger, he wasn't making things easy for punters to pass around each other.

We met up with him again a couple of other times that afternoon and went through the same performance. It was the beginning of a friendship and a source of income that lasted for many years. He didn't confine his activities to racing. During the Italian/Abyssinian war he acted as an ambassador for his country. He stood outside the Rubbing House, talking as well as any politician, but with a difference. He used the ripest language to describe the Italians, and the atrocities he said they were committing. The crowd loved it, and egged him on to the foulest heights, roaring with laughter as he took his cue from them. The coppers, who with any other bloke would have had him in charge, just smiled and walked away. He didn't allow politics to interfere with his business, for when he'd got the crowd well with him, he slipped easily and quickly into his usual routine.

Another famous tipster was a bloke we knew as Gully. He used to shout, 'Gully, gully, gully, gully', to get the crowd around him. He dressed like a bank manager, smart blue suit, cut-away collar, club tie, horn-rimmed spectacles with, as his props, a brief case and rolled umbrella. He'd choose where he was going to stand, peel six or seven fivers off a roll of notes, put them on the grass, and stick them to the ground with his brolly. When he'd got a crowd around him, he'd pull out an apple and start juggling it around, all the time going on about the secret information he had. He'd have someone planted in the crowd, who at a given signal would shout, 'How secret is this bloody information of yours?' 'I'll show you,' he'd say. Then, taking a knife from his pocket, he'd cut the apple in half and out of the core would produce a pound note and a list of horses. 'It's as secret as the heart of this apple, and as fruitful for from its seeds, great trees will grow, all from a small investment,' then he would wave the note. 'But it won't cost you a pound, nor ten shillings, not even five bob. Half a dollar is my charge for making you a fortune.' He mesmerized the crowd with his tricks and chatter. To look at him and to listen to him you'd think he owned a string of racehorses. As I got to know him he gave me one or two good tips, though I don't know whether they were the ones he sold, probably not. He did, however, make a name for himself through a horse called Linber Hill. 'You'll never believe it, Phil, but I saw the winner of the Cheltenham Gold Cup running at a point-to-point called Limba Hill, and mark my words he'll be the first home.' This was four months before the race. Everywhere he went he tipped it and when it won at 100–8 he retraced his steps and grateful punters would not only sing his praises but slip him pound notes. He must have had a record year.

Gully indulged in some card sharping as well. In the old days most people travelled to the races by train, they'd set out flush, ready for any kind of gamble and were easily drawn in to a school. Gully got into the racket by accident, or so he told me. He was on a train in his younger days and four sharpers started up a game in his carriage. He was asked if he would like to join a school of pontoon, and being the conjurer and manipulator he was, he soon discovered they were cheating him, so he decided to take over. By the time the train had reached his destination, the biters had been well and truly bitten. He was able to work this swindle on a number of the gangs, but eventually they got to know him, and as they couldn't beat him he was asked to join. It was lucky for one of our young stable lads that he did, for one day the boy fell in with a school, and had twenty quid taken off him. He told me about it, and I took him along to see Gully. 'Tell me what they look like,' he asked, and matey obliged. 'Yes, that fits, I know 'em. Now don't you worry, sonny, I'll get your money back.' About a week later I met Gully again and he asked for the lad. When I told him he wasn't with me, he handed me an envelope. 'There are four fivers in there, they coughed up all right.' I asked him if he'd had any trouble getting the money. 'None at all. When they heard who and what he was, they came through with it straight away. Dog doesn't bite dog in the racing game.'

Before the security net was drawn tight round race courses, every trainer could employ a spiv to do jobs and run errands for him at any meeting. Some of these were locals, others would travel the racing circuits. They fiddled their way on to the course carrying a bucket or an empty colour bag, shouting some trainer's name at the chap on the gate. They'd do any odd thing, helping the trainer with the saddling, rinsing horses' mouths out, sponging their eyes and nostrils. If a horse was successful, they'd rush into the winning enclosure with the sheet over their arms, looking as if part of his success was down to them. These things were done in the hope of getting a backhander, which eventually found its way to a bookie's satchel. The spivs varied in type. 'Wigan', who must have had a real name but I don't suppose more than half a dozen people ever knew it, was a northerner of about fourteen stone, with a deep bass voice. He was a bird and animal impersonator.

Gefford Brown was a gentleman spiv who came straight out of the pages of the *Tailor and Cutter*. He looked and spoke like an officer and a gentleman. He taught me how to travel the railways free. He'd buy a platform ticket, and when he got to the barrier follow a party through, chatting at them from behind, although he didn't know them from Adam, making it look as if he was seeing them off. The first few minutes of the journey he would spend in the corridor; when he saw a bloke going into the lavatory, he'd start calling 'tickets please' and would knock on the lavatory door. 'Just shove it under the door, sir,' he'd say. As like as not the bloke would do as he'd been told. Gefford would scarper quick with probably a return ticket in his hands. When I first made his acquaintance, I complimented him on the way he dressed, and asked why he did it. 'I'm courting, Phil,' he replied. 'She may be anywhere and everywhere. Her name's Lady Luck, and when I find her, I'd like her to feel I'm fit to greet her.'

Arthur Freeman and Barney Reece were spivs who worked for the bookies. They'd mingle with the lads to try and get us to tell them of our horses' chances. They didn't particularly want the winners, they wanted to know whether a horse was trying or not. If it wasn't, there didn't seem to be much wrong in us telling them, but for a bookie this was useful information, since he could lengthen his odds and take what money he was able to. Of course accidents happened, and they'd be caught with their trousers down.

Professional punters were anxious to know when we had a horse going in, but a stable lad had to be certain of his man before passing information on to him. If the trainer found out, the lad could be in very serious trouble, even get the sack. I was not worried therefore when I was introduced to a gentleman by a close friend from another stable, and told he was both generous and reliable. As it happened, we had one which had been got ready for the next date and since I knew that we'd already placed our bets, I was able to give it to him. It duly won at 7–1, and as my mate had told me that he was the sort of bloke that bet in fifties or hundreds, I reckoned I could look forward to around twenty or thirty quid as a backhander. After the race I went looking for him. It was always as well to get in quick while the punter was relishing his success. I didn't catch him until nearly the end of the meeting. ''allo sir,' I said, 'the old horse did the trick then.' 'Yes,' he replied. 'But to tell you the truth, I didn't have a penny on him. I was on my way to back it, when a head lad gave me another to beat him and like a fool I did that one instead.' 'A likely bloody story,' I thought as I went away with my tail between my legs. After the meeting I saw the stable lad that had introduced me and gave him my thoughts about his pal. 'You're right, he's a bloody liar,' he told me. 'I saw him lay a big bet on myself.' I was determined that if the opportunity ever came my way I would get my own back.

As it happened it came the following week at Sandown. Up comes matey, all smiles and good fellowship and asks if I've got a winner for him. 'Gawd,' I thought, 'the cheek of the idle rich.' I was ready for him. 'As a matter of fact we have got one going,' and I gave him a horse that was a stumer. We'd brought it down for the ride, it hadn't a chance, nor had we any intention that it should come anywhere. Matey went away, pleased as punch, came back a few minutes later, 'Are you sure this is off? There's no money for it in the ring,' 'No,' I said, 'We're backing it SP, we're hoping to get a better price that way.' He was now really convinced that he was on to a good thing. I followed him and had a bet on another horse, which I'd heard was a near certainty.

Then what happened? Ours won. It wasn't a thousand to one chance yet, it skated home. To my surprise Harold Wallington, then my governor, was all smiles, which made me suspicious. I wondered if he'd known all the time that it was going in. 'What're you so chirpy about?' I asked. 'Did you know something I didn't?' 'No, Phil, I didn't have a penny on him, neither did the owner, but his wife ignored his advice and had seventy quid on the horse. She now thinks that owning a racehorse is lovely, and this has made everyone happy.' I brightened a bit since I knew I should get a present from the owner. As I was going to the weighing-room to fetch the colour bag, lo and behold who should appear but matey the punter, grinning all over his face. 'Hey, Phil,' he called out, and I went over to him. He put a bunch of fivers in my hand, and thanked me for what had been one of the best bets of his life. It was the beginning of a beautiful friendship. From then onwards I let him know whenever a horse of ours was trying. It was a profitable partnership, and one I was particularly grateful for during the winter when life was a bit rough. Even if I'd nothing for him, he'd drop me the occasional tenner, a sweetener some cynic might call it, but it was more than most of the other leeches that clung on to stable lads ever did.

One of my earliest punters was a man whom I never saw on a racecourse. I was taking a horse called Zane Grey to Worcester. The first part of the journey was by horsebox from Epsom to Euston, where we transferred to rail. It was an old fashioned box and a horse could stick his nose out of the back. We'd got as far as Clapham Common when the engine packed in. The driver went to phone Mr Richmond for a replacement, leaving me in the cab to worry whether we were going to make it in time. I noticed a gent peering into the box at the horse. He tapped on the window and we started chatting. He said he didn't know anything about racehorses, but was interested in them and started asking questions. The inevitable one came, did I think it was going to win, and I was able to say truthfully that he stood a very good chance. When the driver came back, the gent started to move off, then paused, opened his wallet and handed me a card. 'If it does win, write to me at that address,' he said.

We got to Worcester by the skin of our teeth and Zane Grey won. It wasn't until about a fortnight later that I came across matey's card. I turned it over a few times before deciding to drop him a line. He replied by return, enclosing a fiver, and suggested that if ever I knew of any other likely winners, I should write to him. This wasn't too easy since I had to know a couple of days in advance. Still I was occasionally able to oblige and his generosity continued over the years. Eventually, just before the war, he invited Cath and me to the theatre to see 'The Little Dog Laughed'. He gave us the best seats and a slap-up supper afterwards. He never let on what he did, but since his address was Wardour Street, I think he must have been something in films.

As I've said, trainers didn't want stable lads passing information to punters, or to anyone else for that matter. This is understandable, particularly in a gambling stable where a trainer is making the best part of his living from the bets he has on his horses. For the stable lad, therefore, it was a matter of choosing your punter. Any lad who told someone who was likely to pinch the price was being disloyal and deserved everything that came to him. It happened in Wallington's stable when I was a head lad. We'd got Alf's Caprice ready to win the Victoria Cup, and one of our blokes sold out on us to a villain, who the moment the book opened, stepped in and took as much as he could about the horse, so that when the owner and the governor went in he was almost favourite.

There was a stable inquiry and the lad was sacked. Another of our boys, who was only doing it in a small way, had been sending letters to a punter advising him on horses to back. He had had a bad run and the punter, thinking he was being done over, wrote to Harold and shopped him. It was too near the Victoria

Cup incident for Wallington to be lenient and the boy had to go. But I couldn't see any wrong in passing information in a small and careful way. We were always underpaid and any extra was manna from heaven. It was also common knowledge that a number of trainers had risen from the ranks as a result of the money they'd got out of grateful punters.

If I've one regret in my life, it is that I didn't have the courage of my convictions. I never made a real punter, I just hadn't the nerve. If I had, I could have been a much richer man. Apart from St Andrew the Second, on which I gambled my savings so that I could get married, I've known horses that unless they fell over were bound to lead past the winning post, many, many of them, yet when it came to a gamble the most I would risk was a fiver or a tenner.

Bookies are a much maligned breed. Apart from my boxing days, I never had any direct dealings with them. I was never knowingly used by them as a source of information. They hold a most peculiar position in the racing game for whenever there's any rumour of doing away with them and only using the tote system, punters scream that this would take away the colour and vitality of the racing scene. Bookies are their heroes, yet when they are having their wagers, they are the punters' sworn enemies and they love nothing better than some juicy fraud case involving them. Then all of them suddenly become a bunch of crooks. Yet I reckon that the percentage of honest bookies is high. When I first went into racing there was the odd racecourse gang which ran 'protection rackets' for bookies on the course. The chief of these was the Messina Gang who operated mainly in the south. They preyed on the bookmakers, some of whom found they had to engage their own bully-boys as protection from the gang. Not unnaturally fights broke out, and the blame was shared by both sides. This was unfair as was discovered when the police stepped in and broke up the gang. Attempts were made to harrass the bookies in other small ways. I've seen tough customers standing by a bookie, screaming that they've been cheated, haven't been paid out. What punter is going to use the bookie when he hears that? The bookie pays up and the villains get away with a quid in their hand and move on to upset someone else. The bookie has no option, if he puts in a couple of his own strong men he's up for assault, whether he's in the right or not.

There were also those 'bookies' I saw as a lad, standing at the roadside carrying a blackboard and easel with the sign 'Honest Joe Bloggs' and thumbing a lift to a nearby meeting. They were usually three or four spivs who'd pooled their resources and were off to try their luck, taking bets instead of collecting them. At that time any one could put up a board, no licence was required. The boys worked on the principle that no bookie ever went skint, but generally ended up proving that there was a first time for everything. It was a common sight to see them having to welsh and being chased by a crowd of angry punters, who though they knew they had no chance of getting their money, wanted some sort of run for it. People like this didn't help the reputation of the professional turf accountant.

Trainers regarded bookies in two lights. They were either the villains who tried to squeeze information from their lads, or the bankers who provided the bread when the stable had a gamble. You can't expect to have it both ways, so who's to blame bookies if they try to protect themselves with a first-class communication system. I've known a head lad come up to me a week or so before a big race, and tell me that he's just had a word with his governor and that they've decided to withdraw their horse because he's got a bit of a leg. Then ten minutes later, I've seen that the anti-post bookmakers have pushed their prices on that horse out from ten to one to forty to one. It's nothing short of miraculous how they get to know. Occasionally, one bookmaker will learn that something's gone wrong with a horse, that the trainer is keeping him in for a week trying to get him right but that he doesn't hold out much hope that the horse will run. He keeps the information to himself for as long as he can, and takes as much money as possible, knowing full well that the horse is almost certainly a non-runner. Bookies also attract bad debtors, and with little help from the law they've had to devise their own system in order to avoid being cheated. It works, for any man owing a substantial amount will find it impossible to place a bet anywhere along the line or on the rails. He may get away with a cash bet at a betting shop, but not on the course. It's very rare that a bookie will cheat a punter, it is as much as his living is worth if he's found guilty. Tattersalls have a committee which settles any arguments and there's a Ring Inspector to examine any on-the-spot complaints. Mistakes can happen, but generally complaints occur through wishful-thinking on the punter's part.

Like everything else in racing, bookmaking has changed a lot over the years. The big combines have taken over. Still, it's worth remembering that William Hill founded his organization by laying bets on the Autumn Double, the Caesarewich and Cambridgeshire races six months before they were run. Today it is as if the computer runs the book and the expression 'turf accountant' has become a more accurate one, since 'balancing the books' is now the rule. Before the war I've seen men go up to a bookie on the rails and put £1000 on a horse by word of mouth only, and have it accepted easily and with thanks. Today if you try and hand over £200 or £300 the bookie's hands start to shake and he'll probably only accept a part of it.

It may seem strange but I believe that bookmakers have helped to keep racing clean. Whenever they suspect they're being defrauded, they squeal and they squeal loudly. They don't go running to the police because police procedure is too slow, and the excitement has died down, the money's been lost and the villains have either got away or covered themselves so that prosecution is useless. The bookies therefore have their own security network. Payment is stopped on all bets, an inquiry is immediately put in motion from which they're able to tell in a matter of hours if there has been foul play, and where there has they can quickly present a case for prosecution and hand it to the law. I'm not criticizing the police in saying this, but it's just that bookies know immediately where to look and their methods are not hampered by regulations or red tape. So effective have these methods been over the years that frauds are a rarity.

Great play is made by the racing novelist of the expression 'stopping a horse' as if it's something that gangs of crooks do to nobble the favourite. In fact it's something that happens regularly in stables on the instructions of the trainers. It does not usually happen with class horses, they are got ready for particularly important races, though even they must not come into their peak condition too soon and sometimes have to be kept back. It is more the practice for animals entered in the smaller meetings. A trainer prepares a horse for a particular race and although he wants to give it some practice on a course, he doesn't want its qualities to be seen until he's ready. He has to be careful, as there are people watching for this sort of behaviour, and if a horse runs out of character, he can be in all sorts of trouble. It's hard for the authorities to prove when horses have been stopped, for like human beings, they're entitled to have their off-days, and the buggers do, otherwise there would be such things as racing certainties.

In stables there are generally two ways of stopping horses. The first is to cut down on training. If this is done, the animal should go well for most of the race but when the pressure is on, he'll blow up, run out of gas and fall back. You can read it in the form book: 'Not backed, fair at the distance, disappeared quickly.' Clever punters try following horses like that, they watch them improve, then they try and get inside the trainer's mind to discover exactly when he's going to put them in. Many times I've been asked when I worked in both Smythe's and Wallington's stables, 'When's your guvner going to let that one go?' They didn't expect a definite answer, but they thought they might find out something from the way I replied. The other way of stopping a horse, or as one head lad I knew described it, 'not assisting it too willingly', was through his feed. We would double his hay overnight and feed him up with a big bran mash instead of dry corn, carrots and the normal vitamins. 'Fill him up, blow him out and he can't do his best no matter how hard he tries', was the saying, but once again, nothing is certain in racing.

I remember taking a horse, Rao Sahib, to a Wincanton meeting. He ran and won. Towards the end of the day the fog came down so I rang Harold Wallington and told him we couldn't get the horse back home and that he'd have to stay in the stables that night. Since I always rewarded an animal that had done well, I had given him an extra large feed, both evening and morning. The next day, just as Mick Dillon, the box driver and I were about to move off, the yard manager called out that my governor was on the phone. Harold told me that he had the horse entered in a race at the same meeting that day and that he'd forgotten to withdraw him. 'He'll have to run again, Phil,' he said. I told him I'd over-fed him, that he'd incurred a seven pound penalty through his win the day before and was bound, therefore, to run badly. 'He'll just have to take his chance,' was the governor's reply. Take his chance! He walked the race, won by twice the distance he had the day before against a better field; although I don't need to say it, I didn't have a penny piece on him.

Much has been written about jockeys arranging races. Today it would be well-nigh impossible as the camera's on them from start to finish, and any way who's got the money to make it worth the jockey's while to put his career at stake. The only way a rider might help is by getting left at the start, though the stalls that have now been introduced make this difficult. There have, of course, been real crooks in the game. If there hadn't, there wouldn't have been so many rules and regulations, or such tight security. Many of the cases that have been uncovered have become racing history. I can only speak with any authority on those where I knew the people concerned.

One was particularly notorious and involved Percy Bailey, a small Epsom trainer, who I think was the 'fall-guy' in the affair. He was approached by the villains of the piece to take in two horses, which they'd bought in France. The poorer of the two was entered for a race at Bath but the animals were switched, and the better horse duly won. If the villains had been happy to take a reasonable profit, they might have got away with it. But they were greedy, they had large bets placed all over the country, and to ensure that the price was right they had decided to cut the telephone lines of the blower system. This meant that the bookies at Bath had no idea of the heavy wagering that was going on and so the price of the horse was kept high. Again, if whoever had cut the line had done it properly the result might have been different, but the cut had been made too obviously deliberately, so that when the bookies began to squeal, their cries were acted upon. All bets were held over except to those punters who were paid out on the course, and they could only have been very small and made in complete innocence, while a full inquiry was begun. Billy Gilchrist was the jockey involved, but he made nothing out of it, for if the big boys didn't benefit, it wasn't likely that he would. I commiserated with Percy Bailey afterwards, who though we all knew he was an innocent victim, lost his licence. 'I knew nothing about it, Phil, to tell you the truth all I had was ten bob on him on the tote and they've taken away my good name and my living.' The only person I knew who did get something out of it was George Forbes, the vet. The two horses were kept in his yard for months while the police were collecting evidence before the case finally went to court.

A notorious villain was Ringer Barry, who got his nickname

through ringing the changes on horses. He would even paint one horse to look like another. He was hired to do it by crooked trainers. Another gang found two horses who were almost identical, though one had a white patch on his forehead. It was the one they knew could win, so they ran it in an Australian bridle which has cross bands down to the bit and hid the patch. This was discovered and the swindlers ended up in prison. Crimes of this kind prompted the authorities to insist that every horse has a passport. Today each one is vetted, every distinguishing mark noted, even down to a whirl, for horses are the same as humans and have double crowns, though on various parts of their bodies. Any racecourse vet can check a horse against his passport so ringing is virtually impossible.

When I was working in Wallington's yard, I was surprised to be visited by a couple of detectives, one of whom was looking a bit worse for wear. They asked to see the governor, but he was away at a meeting, so they said I'd do. They wanted me to talk about a stable lad who'd been apprenticed to us, and asked if I knew him, and what my opinion was of him. To be honest, even if I'd thought him a bit of a villain I don't think I'd have told them, but I was able in truth to say that he'd been a first-class worker and as straight as they came. 'Did you ever suspect him of doping a horse?' one of them asked. It knocked the wind out of my sails. 'He'd never dope a horse, they were his life, he loved them.' Again this was true, he used to spend half his wages on titbits for them. 'Well he's been caught and charged with doping horses, and he's admitted it.' Apparently he was one of a gang who had been raiding stables and nobbling fancied horses. He was caught in John Beary's yard near Lambourne. All I could say after that was that I was surprised and that it was completely against the character of the man as I knew him. The coppers didn't seem to like this and I thought they began eyeing me a bit suspiciously. Then the one with the black eye asked me if I'd ever known him to be violent. Again, with my hand on my heart, I could say no. 'Well, it may surprise you to know he did this to me,' and then pointed to his face. 'But he's half your size,' I said. 'Sure you didn't run into a lamp-post?' The copper wasn't amused and showed it, but there was nothing he could do about it so the two of them left. The lad had to go to prison, though he's doing quite well for himself now. I don't agree with what he did, but I have a certain admiration for his daring. It takes a brave man just to break into a box at night and to go in on a strange horse who, if he's frightened, will start kicking out and rearing up and is likely to do him all kinds of damage. But to try and stick a needle into the horse demands even greater courage. As I said, he had a way with horses.

Boidy Davis was a crafty trainer who used dope. He was an Australian who got his nickname because he said that he trained his horses to the whistle, like men do sheepdogs. On a gallop or on the course he had one dangling from his neck on a piece of string and when he wanted his horse to go, he'd blow it, and the animal would take off. It was surprising how many people believed him. He hoped to deceive the stewards when a horse that han't previously shown any form cantered in first at the post. It became obvious though that he was doping his horses and in the end he was rumbled, but he got away with it for far too long. Herbert Smythe made one of his few mistakes when he bought one of Boidy's horses at auction. Potage wasn't worth a wank, as the saying goes. The governor would scratch his head and say, 'How that bloody man won a race with this horse, I'll never know.' Even when he learned that Boidy was giving his horses the old gee-up, Herbert still puzzled. 'I wouldn't have thought there was a drug invented that could make this bugger go.'

At that time Herbert wasn't beyond helping a horse on its way, though he never used drugs that might harm an animal or cause it to hurt a jockey. He kept a regular supply of what he called 'John Haig's tonic'. He had it made up by a chemist in Epsom, and it did do that little bit extra. We lads proved this, for some evenings before going to the Bull Ring we'd have a quick swig from the bottle and it made us feel six foot high.

With jumpers Herbert would have a small bottle of Scotch in his back pocket and an hour before the race tip it down the horse's throat: the horse would go in, wouldn't look behind, and jumped like a good trooper. Also it made a deal of difference to the prop and cop horses, those that went to a fence thinking, 'Shall I or shan't I?', and ended up turning arse over head. After the bottle they'd go straight for a fence and that way they gave the jockey a safer ride. Herbert also thought beer was a good tonic for after a race. He kept a barrel of Burton XXX and would come out to the lad that was doing the horse over with a pint in a small saucepan. ''ere, give the old bugger this with his feed,' he'd say. At least half of it generally found its way down the lad's throat, until Herbert rumbled what was happening. He put a stop to it by mixing a spoonful of ground ginger in with the beer. Today it would be impossible to give a horse any form of alcohol in time for it to affect his form, for a urine test would show it. You're not allowed to administer any type of medicine either; if a horse is sick and you've declared it, you can withdraw him by producing a vet's certificate.

Once without being aware of what he was doing, Herbert ran a drugged horse. It was decided on the morning of the day he was racing that Big Ben should be tubed. It was an operation performed on animals that 'die' on you, that is run out of breath in the last few hundred yards. A circle of flesh was cut out of the larynx and a metal pipe inserted so that the air went straight into the horse's windpipe. The pipe could be closed so that normally the horse was breathing as usual, but when he was racing it was open and he'd be able to get a full rush of air. Before cutting the flesh, the vet injected cocaine into the throat to stop the pain. The operation was simple and little blood was lost. Mr Markham, Herbert's vet, did an excellent job and Big Ben went off to the meeting all merry and bright. The governor hadn't fancied him strongly, but he had a fair bet on him, and he won. That evening, when Mr Markham came to look at the horse, Herbert congratulated him on his work and told him the good tidings. 'I'm not surprised he won,' the vet said, 'I reckon even you would have walked it with that amount of cocaine in your body.'

One trick that both Smythe and Wallington resorted to often deceived the eye. If we had a horse that won a selling plate race as a two-year-old and we thought we could safely have a gamble on him the following year, we'd put him by for a spell, just giving him an outing from time to time, but with no thought of winning with him. Then, towards the end of the year, the trainer would look for a seller that the horse could win. Now, since we intended having it off with him, it was no good taking him to the course looking in top condition, the knowledgeable punters and the bookmakers would remember the previous win and any gamble would fail.

Around the end of September or the beginning of October stables gave the horses what they called the 'blackberry clip' to

106

make them look smart for the rest of the season. If they were not going to run any more that year, their coats could grow, so that nature kept them warm. Their manes wouldn't be pulled and their tails could grow longer. In the same way you'd leave the horse you hoped to win alone and send him to the meeting looking almost scruffy. You'd also fit his legs with a couple of surgical bandages with plenty of cotton wool spilling over the top or, if it was a trick you hadn't tried too often, you'd use Poudre Ambrocaine. Applied to a horse's leg some three or four days before a race, then washed off, this changed the colour of his hair so it was clear that something had been put on the legs. If you did either of these things, when the horse was walking around in the ring people would say 'Hallo, that horse looks as if it's got a bit of an "if"', which meant that there was probably something wrong with the leg or a tendon.

If the trainer wanted to take the deception further, he'd have another horse from his own stable entered along with it. This horse would have been clipped and smartened up for the occasion, and would be wearing a brand new paddock cloth, whereas the intended winner would carry an old set. Now the ordinary race-goer would be in no doubt that the smart-looking horse was the one intended to win, while even the most experienced professional punter would be in two minds. He might even have come to the meeting especially to back the shabby one, remembering its performance as a two-year-old, and knowing something of the reputation the stable had for bringing off a gamble. But those punters don't like ifs or buts, they want to be as nearly certain as possible before chancing their money. The secret of their success is that they are prepared to wait, so more likely than not they will leave it alone. If there's no real money coming for the horse, the bookies will let the price go out and the stable gamble is made. Obviously this is something that can't be done too often. In the stables where I've worked, we've only had it off four times.

Another worry with selling plates is that you may not want to lose the horse at the auction afterwards, since you know he's likely to be more successful. Again, the surgical bandages and the Poudre Ambrocaine help to deceive a potential buyer. He may think that you've put the horse in knowing that his legs are tricky, and that the stable will be glad to get shot of him. On each seller, there is a figure fixed below which the animal will not be sold. Any money that is reached above this figure is divided half and half between the racecourse authorities and the owner of the horse that comes in second. It therefore stands to reason that the first person a winning trainer approaches is his opposite number who is looking after the runner up. They get together and agree a figure that is to be paid if the trainer of the second horse doesn't enter the bidding.

The thinking behind this is that even if the owner of the second horse doesn't particularly want the horse but starts bidding to increase his cut, those around the ring will believe he's after the animal because, knowing his own to be good, he realizes he's on to a better. Generally an agreement can be reached because the trainer of the second horse realizes that one day he may need a similar arrangement. If there's no settlement and he buys the horse, then trouble can start. Harsh words are spoken and frequently blows exchanged. The practice is of course frowned upon by those in authority, but they don't interfere, wisely I think, unless there's been intimidation.

Only once have I had to buy a horse in. It was on the day when Jimmy Lindley rode Bowral Boy for us at Worcester. The governor wasn't at the meeting because he felt that if he showed his face it would affect the gamble he was taking. 'If it wins, buy it in for two hundred quid, but not a penny more,' were his instructions. The horse was entered to be sold at £100, so this meant that I could only spend another hundred. Bowral Boy went well and Jimmy headed Gordon Richards into second with ease. Before the race I went to the auctioneer and told him that we thought the horse stood a good chance, that we wanted him back, and that I would be leading him round if he won and bidding for him. I asked his advice. 'I'll be looking for you, just give a slight nod of the head when you want to come in,' he told me. I was nervous as I was going towards the sale ring, so I was not pleased when I was stopped by three men. 'He won like a goodun, didn't he boyo,' one said to me, while the others looked the horse over. 'He surprised us today, still we'll be glad to be shot of him,' I said. 'Likely to do well for us flapping down at Neath.' I didn't answer but got the horse to the ring and just hoped I'd put some doubt into their minds.

The bidding duly started at £100 and went up to £200 with

these Welshmen against me. I knew everyone was curious to know who was bidding against them, and that if the men thought the stable was trying to buy him in, they were likely to go higher, but seeing me moving around with the horse confused them. Somehow I had the feeling that the auctioneer was on my side, perhaps he'd acted on the information I'd given him and had a good bet. Still the bidding had now gone to £200 and that was the governor's limit. I decided to go out on a limb. I felt Bowral Boy was too good a horse to let go at that price, and I didn't fancy him falling into the hands of those Welshmen. I was lucky, he only cost me another £20. As I led him out of the ring, the trio came up to me. 'Who bought him then? We didn't see anyone bidding.' 'I did,' I said, 'for the stable.' 'You lying little sod, you said you'd be glad to see him go.' 'That was before I knew you were after him.'

I stayed the night at Worcester but didn't ring Harold Wallington as I'd been told to do. I didn't want a rollocking over the phone for over-bidding. I needn't have worried, for the next day he'd seen the news in the *Sporting Life* and so had the owner, Bertie Kerr, an Irish horse dealer. They'd both had a good bet and were pleased they'd have a chance with the horse again. The man who was happiest with the result, I think, was young Jimmy Lindley although he hadn't had a penny on the animal. For him it was another rung up the long and slippery ladder which he eventually climbed to the top.

I hope punters aren't distressed by this chapter. If they are, I can offer them no comfort, as I've only written about my own experience. I do know how difficult it is to pick a decent winner if you're on the course every day and you study the form book all night. How then can men really hope to win sitting in the pub reading the papers, or standing in the betting shops or watching the television. It's impossible. I also know that by saying this I shan't make the slightest difference to any bookie's takings. After all, there are just as many people falling for the three-card trick now as there were in my granddad's day.

6

*Joining the union – Parting company with Herbert Smythe –
Harold Wallington, head lad, to the rescue – St Andrew II: saint
or devil? – John Nightingall, trainer – St Andrew is exorcised –
Rigging a gallop – A racing certainty – Glorious Goodwood with
our shirts on the line – Sweetness and gall*

It was a fine autumn evening the back end of 1936. I was in
stables doing my horse over. My thoughts were anywhere, for
when the job is one you've done morning and evening every day
for nine years, you can do it in your sleep. I'd set him fair and was
dressing him over when I sensed that someone was standing behind me in the doorway. I knew it must be Herbert Smythe; I
reckoned I could tell when he was twenty yards away. I began
polishing and brushing at double speed, not that it really mat-
tered, for however fast I worked, it was seldom quick enough or
good enough for him.

I could feel him watching me. My arms now began to ache.
'Whatever it is you've got to say, let's 'ave it,' I thought. 'So
you've joined the union 'ave yer?' he snarled at last. 'Yes, sir.'
'D'yer know what it means?' 'Yes, sir.' 'It means yer a bloody
commy, that's what it means.' Even in those days communism
was a dirty word, so it got my rag up. 'That's not true and you
know it.' 'So you're calling me a liar, you bleedin' little sod –
after all I've done for you over the years – all I've taught you.'
'You've done nothing for me that didn't suit yerself, and it's cost
yer bugger all,' I threw back at him though I could see it was one
of those arguments that wasn't going to get anywhere. 'So that's
what you think, you little bastard.'

That was enough for me. I turned back to my horse, picked up
his rug, threw it across him, did up the straps carefully and
patted his neck. 'Goodbye old fella,' I whispered in his ear.

'Christ,' I thought, 'this is like one of those western pictures.' I walked over to the stable door. 'Excuse me, sir.' The governor stepped to one side. I thought he might try and clout me as I went past him, but I was ready for it if it came. 'Well then, it's goodbye, I'm off.' And I walked across and out of the yard where I'd worked since I was a boy of thirteen. I waited for him to call me back – he wouldn't have apologized. He didn't know the meaning of the word, but I didn't think he'd let me go just like that. I felt I was too useful to him. I was wrong.

I suppose it was this that hurt me more than his words had. I began calling myself all sorts of a bloody fool for jacking my job in. And for what? For joining a union that wasn't even properly started. It had no powers. All right, some lads at Lambourne had gone on strike for better conditions. They'd set their horses loose to wander over the fields and the roads and they'd refused to go back until they'd got what they thought were their rights. But they'd gone back and rumour had it they were worse off then they had been before. In any case, I couldn't see myself or any of our lads letting horses free to roam round the streets of Epsom and possibly getting themselves hurt or worse. They meant too much to us. They had to or we wouldn't be doing the job.

Yet it had all seemed to make sense the day before at the recruitment meeting at the Railway Inn in the Upper High Street. All for one and one for all. Unity means strength. Old Bill Bromley the pub owner, who was a trainer himself, was all for it. He looked after the horses that raced as trotters at Northolt. The course didn't come under Jockey Club, only Pony Turf Club rules. It wasn't a licensed track in the true sense of the word and had its own sets of rules and code of conduct – you got away with what you could as long as you weren't found out. So I thought perhaps after all Bill Bromley's words weren't worth all that much. Perhaps he was encouraging us so as to spite the other real trainers who looked down on him. Still, there was no backing out of it now. I'd gone along with all the other lads. I'd paid my dues – a bob a week – and got my badge. That set me off on another track. Would our lads come out on strike when they knew what had happened to me? 'Not bloody likely they won't,' I thought. Anyway, I'd walked out, I hadn't been sacked, and I wouldn't want them out. It was personal. Something between Herbert and myself.

111

My thoughts had taken me to my lodgings. 'You're back early,' said Auntie, as I went in. 'Is Manch with you?' 'No he's not, Auntie' I replied. I must have sounded like I felt, because she looked at me hard. 'Something wrong?' she asked. 'I've just packed it in with the guvner.' 'Packed it in? Why? What was up?' I told her the story. She walked over to the living-room door, took her coat off the hook and started to put it on. 'I'll soon sort that old bugger out,' she said. And she would have. 'No,' I said. 'Not this time. I've had enough. I'm going home.' 'You don't want to go home after what you've learnt all these years. You know the game now. You may as well stick with it. Besides, your mum and dad'll be disappointed.' 'Well,' I said, 'I'll think it over. Give it till tomorrow,' – it was a Saturday. 'If I can't find a way out, I'll go home on Sunday. But I don't want you interfering. I must sort this one out myself.'

When Manch came in, I told him about it. He understood too. He didn't offer any advice, he just knew it was my business. 'I s'pose you'll be going into town to tell Cath.' 'Yes,' I said. Telling her was going to be the hardest thing of all. We had been going steady for the last five years and were saving up to get married. I hadn't got very far – £30 was all I had in the world. I knew she would take it hard and probably try and get me to eat humble pie to Herbert. Still, I thought, if I went home I wouldn't be far away. We could still see each other regularly. I'd still want her. But then, would she want me – I knew enough about women to know that absence doesn't necessarily make the heart grow fonder. One thing I was certain of, her mum and dad would think it good news.

Manch must have guessed my thoughts. 'Why don't you leave it till tomorrow, you may have sorted things out by then.' I jumped at the chance to put it off. Instead, he and I went out for a drink together. It was a waste of money. It didn't do anything for me. I must have been bad company that night. We sat in the pub like a couple of zombies gazing into our beer. When I got into bed, I kept reliving the scene I'd had with Herbert. One thing was certain, I couldn't go back unless the old man came for me. If I did, he'd squeeze the life blood out of me. Then I knew I wouldn't be able to get into any other stables, not in Epsom at any rate. The trainers might compete with each other on the course, they might even be envious and jealous, but they were as

112

one in their behaviour towards their staff. No one would step out of line by offering better wages or conditions, and it was certain that no one would take me on once the governor had told his side of the story, even though they might know in their hearts it wasn't true. So there was nothing for it but for me to pack up, go home and become a fishmonger. The trouble was I didn't want fishmongering. I wanted horses, and Auntie had been right about mum and dad being disappointed. Although I was still a stable lad, in their eyes I was a jockey, and from what they told the neighbours, you'd have thought I was a young Gordon Richards. For me to go back home now and say I'd decided to pack the game in, would only mean one thing – I'd failed, that I was washed-up. I suppose it's true to say that that night was the nearest I ever came to crying myself to sleep.

The next morning I woke as usual at half-past five for work at six o'clock. Manch was getting out of bed. I was about to do the same. 'You don't have to get up you know.' Manch's words hit me and yesterday's events came rushing back. But now I thought, something would turn up. I settled back in bed. I must have dozed off for a time, for I was woken by a knock at the front door. My heart leapt as I heard a man's voice asking if Phil was in. 'The guvner's come round to ask me back,' was the thought that crossed my mind. I opened the bedroom door and went out on to the landing. I could see a man's shape in the doorway. He was wearing jodhpurs, so I knew straight away it wasn't Herbert Smythe. 'Tell him Harold Wallington wants to see him.' Harold Wallington, my heart sank again. He was not someone I knew well. He was travelling head lad for M. D. Blair, the Ewhurst trainer. He wasn't likely to be the bearer of good tidings.

I went downstairs in my pyjamas. ''allo, Phil,' he said, 'I hear you've had an up-and-downer with your guvner.' Gawd, I thought, bad news travels fast in this town. 'That's right,' I said, a bit short so he'd know I wasn't going to talk of it with strangers. 'Well,' he continued, 'while I'm sorry to hear about it, p'raps now you and I can do some business together. I haven't time to explain it all now I've got to get over to Blair's, but I'll tell you the story later. What I want you to do is to get yourself dressed and go up to John Nightingall's stables, I've got a horse there, St Andrew II. I want you to ride him out, I haven't got the time. Will you do it?' Well as there didn't seem anything else for

113

me to do I agreed. 'Good,' he said. 'Now you'll have to move. You know what a funny old bugger John is. He'll want you out of his yard before nine o'clock.' John Nightingall had got religion. He went to morning and evening service every day of his life, a pillar of the Church you might say. Not really the sort of character you'd expect a racing man to be, yet he really knew horses, he and his brother William had both been big figures in the game. When William had died, his son Walter took over and continued the tradition. He had some very good horses indeed, and some big owners, among them Dorothy Paget, Prince Littler and Mrs J. B. Rank. Old John was in his late seventies, but he still had his thumb very much in the pie and regularly every season he had a few winners.

When Harold left, I went upstairs, put on my jodhpurs and five minutes later was making my way over to John Nightingall's yard. I was just in time. The horses were ready to leave. Freddie Broadbent, one of John's senior lads, came over to meet me. ''allo, Phil, so you're riding out St Andrew, this horse of Harold's are yer?' 'So he's just told me.' I said. 'What's he like?' 'He's a bit of a bugger – been roaring and shouting all morning. You'll find him a bit colty too. When I collected him, Frankie Armstrong's lad told me there that though he'd just won this good seller, they'd be glad to be shot of him. He was just a bloody trouble maker. Still, you'll soon be able to find out for yourself, won't you. Go and get your tack on and off we'll go.'

This was not the sort of music I wanted in my ears that particular morning, and I began to wonder what Harold Wallington's game was. I got St Andrew saddled up and took him out into the yard. 'Don't ride too close to our string, them was the old man's instructions, we don't want him coming to any harm,' Freddie Broadbent shouted as we started to move away. 'And remember what I said, he's a bit colty.' That was the understatement of the year. He was a sex maniac. Just as I got out of the gate and onto the road, the United Dairies milk cart came along. St Andrew took one look at the horse pulling it and went berserk. He started rearing and roaring and plunging towards it. The milkman's face went the colour of cream as I struggled to stay with my horse. He recovered quickly because when he got past me he shouted, 'What's that bugger you're riding called, Casanova?' As I was later to find out, he was both right and wrong, for I knew enough to know that Casanova wasn't bent. St Andrew was; no matter what shape or size a horse, whether it was filly, colt or gelding, he wanted to mount it. Still, my immediate job was to get him straightened up a bit. I gave him a few cracks around the behind and we made our way to the Downs. Once up there, he was all right. He cantered, and cantered well.

When we got back to stables, Freddie came up and asked me how he'd gone. 'I reckon he'll be all right,' I said. 'He goes well but he needs straightening out otherwise he'll be hurting somebody, and since that somebody looks like being me, I'll have to see to him.' I looked after him and rode him out morning and evening for the rest of the week. We got on terms, which stopped me thinking about going back to London and being a fishmonger. It looked an even money chance that he would become a goodun, it seemed that one door had shut and another opened. But I hadn't seen or heard anything of Harold Wallington and I was getting restive.

He came round late on Saturday morning. 'How's it going, Phil?' he asked. 'Me, the horse or the money?' I asked. 'Well, let's hear about the horse first. What d'yer think of him?' It seemed to me that it would pay to be careful. 'To tell you the truth Harold, he's a bugger, a real awkward bugger, and he's going to take some sorting out.' I then came out with a list of his faults. When I'd finished he looked a bit crestfallen. 'But how does he go, Phil?' 'He goes well, and I think he'll go a lot better, but it's going to take time, and it's my feeling that's something you're a bit short of for time means money.' I could tell from his expression that I'd hit the nail on the head. 'I can pay you Phil, but not full wages, not yet at any rate.' 'I think I knew that, Harold, but before we talk money, there's other things I want to know.' These were the answers to questions that had been going through my mind all week.

The first question was who owned the horse. I knew it couldn't be Harold. He hadn't got that kind of money, and if it was on the level and there was a proper owner, how was it that that owner hadn't given it to a recognized trainer? Harold was a head lad and a good one, but he hadn't got a trainer's licence. Then where did John Nightingall come in, and why was the horse in his yard? There was something a bit fishy somewhere. I didn't mind bending the rules, I'd got a bit used to that with Herbert Smythe, nor was I in the position of being holy about them, but before I was going to agree to anything, I wanted to know what rules I was going to have to bend.

Harold told me the story from the beginning. It had started when he fell and broke his leg badly riding a villain. He was in hospital and off racing for several months; during this time he decided he wanted out, not of racing, for he knew nothing else, but out of routine stable work and riding. He'd had a few good winners, but he knew he was not likely to make the grade as a jockey. So realizing he was going to get a tidy sum in compensation for his injuries, he began thinking of what he could do to improve things for himself. Sometime after he'd gone back to work, Lady Luck took over. He went to Blackpool, his wife's home town, and was introduced to a Mr Hayes, a local businessman whose ambition was to own a racehorse. Harold promised to look out for one for him and it was agreed that if he found one, he'd look after it.

A few days later he met Stafford Ingham, then a jockey, and told him of his hopes of becoming a trainer. 'You may be just the man I need,' Staff told him. 'I'm thinking along the same lines, though it'll be a year or two before I take the plunge, but I'm getting ready for the day and have been looking out for one or two good horses, so that I've something to start with. In fact I've just bought one, you probably saw it running at Epsom in a seller, it's called St Andrew II.' Harold had seen the race and so had I. The horse had beaten a good field, including Fred Hardigan's Blue Boy and another called Guilty.

Staff had had to have someone bid for St Andrew, of course, because as a jockey he wasn't allowed to own a racehorse, and he went on to say that he was now looking for someone as part owner for him and under whose name he could run, so that at least everything would appear to be legal. He was also on the lookout for a trainer, which was where Harold came in, for although John Nightingall was prepared to let Staff use one of his boxes, and act as trainer in name, which again was against the laws, he wasn't prepared to take the horse on. Harold saw this as his golden opportunity. He told Staff about Mr Hayes and agreed to look after St Andrew. They went together to Blackpool where the bargain was struck, with Mr Hayes taking over the major share of the horse.

116

I was still a bit worried. 'Aren't you still taking a bit of a chance? Too many people know about it already. It's bound to leak out to other trainers.' 'It's one I'm prepared to take, Phil. In any case the trainers in Epsom are a close lot, I reckon they'll keep it to themselves as much as for John's sake as for mine, or their own for that matter if ever they want to pull a fast one.'

What Harold said was true. In those days there was loyalty among the racing fraternity and of course the press weren't so busy looking for stories. 'But what about you, Harold?' I asked. 'Aren't you taking one hell of a chance staking all you've got on this one horse?' 'Of course I am, and so are you, but what's the option? If I don't do it when the chance comes along, I'll never do it, and if the gamble doesn't come off, what have I lost – a bit of money that's all. I'll still have my job at Blair's. No, it's now or never. As for you, if it comes off I'll see you all right, you know that. And if it don't, by that time people will have forgotten your difference with Herbert and you'll be able to get a job anywhere.' This brought me round to my other worry, my money. He didn't offer much, still it was just about enough for me to live on. I had a word with Auntie, and she cut my rent for the time being, so though occasionally I did have to dig into my capital, I had a roof over my head and my feet under the table.

For the next week or two it was the same daily routine. Although St Andrew settled down a bit with me, his behaviour didn't change much. Not quick enough for our future hopes. I tried every trick I knew with him. I found out that it was no good hitting him, he just didn't understand why, so played up accordingly. I got some way by talking to him, but I'd have had to have talked myself hoarse to have made any real change. Still, I persevered.

During this time I got to know John Nightingall well, or rather bits of him, those bits that he allowed to show. He was an amiable enough cove on the surface, but he was as mean as one of his church mice. He was a scavenger and he used me as his assistant. It wasn't something I enjoyed, but since Harold had told me that whatever I did I must keep in with John, I became his unwilling servant. On the way back from exercising the horses, he would be gazing around and if his eyes lit on wooden boxes or empty bottles, he'd tell me to pick them up and carry them home. After race meetings were the best or worst times, whichever way you looked at it. The bookies would leave behind the crates they'd been standing on to shout the odds and of course there'd be any number of bottles littered around the Downs. The boxes were used for firewood and for heating up the mash. 'Don't go using any coal until you've burnt all them boxes,' he'd shout at the lads. The bottles were stood in a shed outside to await the regular visit of the rag and bone man. He took a delight in flogging the bloke something he hadn't paid for himself. The funny thing was that none of us thought the worse of John for this streak in his nature. It fascinated us and we were always watching to see what he'd do next to save himself a halfpenny.

It was after three or four weeks had gone by with only a slight improvement in St Andrew's behaviour, that I told Harold the time had come to do some straight thinking. 'Why don't we have him cut?' I said. Harold didn't like the idea at all. 'If he does turn out to be a goodun, we won't be able to have him standing at stud, so we'll lose out on him there.' 'That's all bloody well,' I argued 'but at the rate he's going, he's not likely to have the chance to prove himself.' 'Tell you what, Phil, let's have Bowen Jones to take a look at him before we decide. He may come up with some ideas.' Bowen Jones was one of the local vets and a first-rate man with horses, as most of the vets were at that time. He wasn't one of your present-day types who drives up in a smart suit, even smarter car, takes one look at the animal, gives him a quick jab in the back with a needle, says that'll be £10 and then zooms off to some old lady to do the same to her poodle.

When Mr Jones arrived in the yard, he looked as though he belonged where he was, old twill trousers, dirty old mac with a cap perched on the back of his head. I was on my own with the horse. ''allo, Welsh,' he said, 'that looks like a good one you've got there. What's the matter with him?' He listened carefully to what I had to say. Then he examined him thoroughly. 'Well, Welsh,' he said, 'from what you've told me and what I've seen, he's got what we call red worm.' This was new to me. 'Red worm,' he went on, 'can kill a horse. It gets into the blood stream, affects the heart and eventually, with over-exertion, the animal can drop down dead. Just like a coronary. It's not an easy job to cure it, it's going to mean washing him out. There's a certain amount of risk doing that, so you go back and tell Harold what I've said and if he agrees, I'll come along in a couple of days' time and do

118

it.' Well, Harold didn't like the sound or the expense of it, but as he said, he had no option but to agree.

Bowen Jones came back. He explained about the risk. 'Some vets in the past have got it wrong. Instead of putting the tubing up the horse's nostril and through into the belly, they've put it into the lungs so that when the solution's been pumped in, the horse has drowned.' 'Oh my Gawd,' I said 'You will be careful won't you, sir? A few of us have got our futures staked on him.' He smiled and said, 'I think it'll be all right, Welsh, I've done it a few times now and I've never lost one yet.' Still, I was very uneasy and I watched every move he made. I warned him that the horse could be a villain. He took my meaning and he went at him firmly but gently. It can't be easy putting tubing up even a quiet horse's nostril, even after doing it down with glycerine, but he managed it with St Andrew scarcely stirring, though his eyes were wide open and rolling around like spinning tops.

Mr Jones described everything he did while he was doing it as if I was his student. When the pipe was through his nostril and down near his throat, he watched St Andrew breathing and as he took a breath he pushed the pipe further so that it touched his larynx. This made him swallow in, and as he did so Mr Jones pushed the pipe over that bit of the throat between the wind pipe and the stomach and when it got towards the stomach side, he showed me where the tube was pushing the skin out as he worked it down the throat. When he'd got the length of the pipe into him, he first put the other end of the pipe to his ear and then handed it to me. 'Can you hear his belly rolling?' he asked. I nodded. 'That means it's in the right place. If it was in his lungs he'd just blow wind into your ear.'

He then took the white enamel bucket that he'd brought with him with its mixture of tepid water, linseed oil, Epsom salts and the powder for killing the worms that we'd prepared before-hand, connected the pipe to a small pump and began moving it up and down slowly. This was the moment I expected St Andrew to play up. So did the vet, and both of us started talking softly to him. We were like a couple of pigeons billing and cooing. I think the horse was so taken aback with two men behaving like idiots that he forgot about what was going into his innards the wrong way. When the bucket was empty, Mr Jones pulled the pipe out as gradually as he'd put it in. St Andrew sniffed and snuffled when it was clear but he still stayed quiet. It was as if he knew that we were only trying to help him. 'So far so good, and that's my job finished,' said Mr Jones. 'Now Welsh, get some hot mash down him and we'll wait for the fun to start.' And it did. No sooner had he eaten than it came pouring out from his behind. 'It's bringing those worms with it, or I'm a Dutchman,' the vet said. When the flood had quietened down a bit, he packed up his gear and waded towards the door. 'I think I can leave you to clear up,' he said as he left. 'It's a dirty job but I think you'll find it has all been worth while. I'll come and look at him in a couple of days. You should have seen some improvement in him by then.'

He was right. What that purge did to St Andrew was little short of a miracle. Everything about him changed, his coat, his manner, his temperament and his attitude towards his work. It was as if he was saying, 'I feel on top of the world now. I'm down to business.' He did stay a bit colty but now he was more particular. Not for him the horse in the milk cart or any old hack, but he'd still stop in his tracks if he saw other racehorses on the Downs. When Harold saw the change in him, he was like a child with a new toy. 'Now,' he said, 'we've got to get a gallop. Someone who'll let him go with their horses. John's got nothing good enough here, so I'll see if I can get Walter Nightingall to agree.' A few days later he came up to me and said, 'I've fixed it with Walter, it was a piece of cake. I've entered St Andrew in the Charlton Welter Handicap over a mile at Goodwood and Walter's got a couple in the same race, one he very much fancies, so he's as keen on a gallop as we are. Tell me Phil,' he went on, 'what weight are you?' 'I'm around eight three.' 'Well, I'll make up a bit of weight for you to wear. It'll give me an idea as to how we're handicapped.'

The gallop was arranged for a Saturday morning. While I was in the yard getting St Andrew ready, Harold came up on his bike carrying what looked like a bit of tartan rug. He slung it at me as he came to the box door. 'Here, put that on under your sweater.' I tried to catch it with my fingers, but it went through them and on to the floor. 'Christ, that's heavy,' I said. 'What is it?' 'It's a waistcoat and I've sewn some weights in the pockets.' 'How much?' I asked. 'I dunno. I hadn't any scales handy. I just cut up some pieces of lead sheeting, we'll be able to tell when we get back, but whatever you do, don't let anyone see what you're wearing.' I found when I put the waistcoat on that that was going to be difficult. It was too big for me and the weights came down to my groin, so that when I sat on the horse, they were hanging around my belly and I found it hard to crouch properly. 'How's the horse been going?' Harold asked after I had finally adjusted myself to his liking. 'Like a real goodun,' I told him. 'If I'm any judge he'll take some beating this morning.' 'That's just what he's got to take,' Harold said smoothly. 'What do you mean?' I asked. 'Just what I said. He's got to be beat. If you feel him running away with you, you've got to hold him back. I don't want Walter, or anyone else for that matter, to know how good he is.' I took his meaning. 'Think you can hold him?' he queried. 'Yes, I think I can do that all right. I learnt a thing or two with old Herbert, but with this weight on me, it may not be necessary.' 'Well, let's get up there and see then,' Harold said.

We joined Walter and his string on the Downs. He'd brought along some good ones, both horses and jockeys. Johnnie Gilbert, riding at six twelve, was on Astral Plain; Mick Kelly was on a good mare, Selina, who'd run a race at Sandown the previous week; there was Ethland, a grey, a fair sprinter who later won a couple of races, and Miss Margie Nightingall, Walter's sister, was riding, too, a fine rider in any company. She understood horses as well as any man, as she showed when she took over from Walter in his latter days when he was ill. She was riding Aristocracy, which was the one they fancied in the same race as us at Goodwood. After we'd exchanged greetings, Walter said, 'Well, let's get on with it. Off you go down to the gallop.' Harold just had time for a few last words. 'Remember, Phil, even if you can beat this lot, don't. Tuck him in with them and keep him there, though you can come a bit at the finish so that it looks as though you made a race of it.' Tommy Isaac, the jumping jockey, rode down to the start with us on a hack.

We all got away well and St Andrew had never gone better. I hadn't been on a horse that went so well. Following Harold's instructions I kept him with the others. Towards the finish I felt Miss Margie coming behind me with her horse and I found it difficult holding St Andrew back, but I sat there with one hand tight and the other hooking him back and let her beat me by a length. I trotted up to the top of the gallop and Miss Margie came upsides of me. I can see her now. She was a most unladylike

121

sight, her nose was running with the exertion and as she wiped it on the back of her hand, she said in a squeaky voice, 'You've no bloody chance with us at Goodwood have you, Welsh?' 'No, Miss.' I agreed only too willingly; it was obvious she hadn't seen what I'd been doing to St Andrew. 'Still,' she shrilled grudgingly, 'it's possible you might run into a place.' 'I don't think so, Miss,' I said a bit too quickly, because I saw her take a sharp look at me. I'd better be careful how I play this, I thought. So when I got back to where Harold and Walter were standing and Walter said, 'Aristocracy had you well beat, eh Welsh?' I thought I'd cover myself a bit. 'Yes, but our one's a fair old horse and should win a seller or two.' So with Walter well satisfied and Harold duly grateful to him, we parted company and made for home.

When we'd put a fair distance between us, Harold said, 'Now tell me the real story, Phil.' 'Well, Harold, he could have pissed it. He nearly pulled my arms out.' 'You don't mean it, Phil?' But Harold had caught my mood. He could see that I did. When we got back to the yard and after I'd seen to St Andrew, he said, 'Old John's got some Jockey Club scales somewhere hasn't he?' 'Yes,' I said, 'they're up in the loft.' 'Right, now we'll see what weight you was carrying.' The steps up to the loft were a bit rickety but I'd managed them before without any accidents. This time, when I got to the second step, it gave way beneath me and I nearly broke my leg. 'Christ,' I thought, 'There must be some weight in this waistcoat.' And I was right, for when I got on the scales I went over ten stone. 'Bloody 'ell,' Harold cried, 'look at that, and we're only carrying eight stone thirteen at Goodwood.' 'What's Aristocracy got?' I asked. 'Eight stone.' 'I can't believe it,' I said, 'I could have picked her up and carried her. Yet she's won a couple of good handicaps, and ours has only won a seller.' The two of us started dancing around that old barn. Eventually Harold calmed down. 'Look Phil, I don't have to tell you . . .' I interrupted him. 'No you don't, Harold. I shan't say a word to a living soul.'

As the Goodwood meeting grew nearer, I began to feel the responsibilities hanging heavier on me. I looked after St Andrew as if he was the favourite for the Derby. I hated leaving him alone. It was as much as I could do not to move my bed in with him. On the morning of the race, Albert Wall arrived early with the horse box. St Andrew was in the two o'clock, the first race of the day.

We had an easy run down in good spring weather, but when we got to the yard, George Lawrence greeted me with some astonishment and with the news that no box had been booked for us. John Nightingall hadn't made the necessary arrangements. However, George was helpful. 'Don't worry Phil, I'll get one for you. Mr Varley's got a box that he can spare. I'll ring him and tell him to expect you.' He was as good as his word and I soon had St Andrew bedded down and comfortable. Albert and I then went along to the pub. Over our beers he asked me if I thought the horse had any chance. 'Yes, Albert. I think he's a real humdinger.' 'You going to back him yourself?' 'To tell you the truth Albert,' I said, 'I'm having all I possess on him, and that's twenty five quid.' 'My Gawd,' he said 'you must know something. Well if he's worth all that to you, he must be worth a fiver of mine.' 'Will you put the money on for me?' I asked. He agreed and I handed over five of those lovely white crispy fivers. I felt a bit light-headed as I did it. 'Do you want it on the tote or the book?' he asked. Now I don't want you to think I mistrusted Albert, but if like me you'd been born and bred in South East London, you'd have learned that all men are human. You'd also have learned not to put temptation in anyone's way. I'm not saying that Albert would have, but if I'd said, put it on the book, and he'd struck a bet at say 15–1, and if the horse had won, there would have been nothing to stop him saying that he'd only got 10–1, or if the price fell, even less. I might well be delighted when he told me, but he'd be laughing his head off; whereas with the tote there was only one price and that was declared at the end of the race, so that's where I told him to put the money. 'On the nose or each way?' he queried. 'To win only. It's shit or bust,' I put it bluntly.

We decided to leave early for the course, we were in the first race and we didn't want to get caught up in the traffic on Trundle Hill. When we reached the yard, I met George Lawrence again. He asked me if I fancied St Andrew. I wanted to do George a good turn since he'd done one for me earlier, so I told him I did and the amount of money I was having on him. I suppose I was getting a bit reckless in my talk now, but never having had that kind of money on a horse before, it seemed I wanted to tell the world about it.

I left George and led St Andrew into the ring. Ken Gethin, the Birmingham jockey, was riding for us, as he'd done in the seller at Epsom. Kenny wasn't doing too well for mounts at that time. He was a good jockey, but being a Brummy he was too blunt and straight talking for some of the racing fraternity. He wasn't one of the yes sir, no sir type, forever touching his forelock, but he was a marvellous rider and later came very much in demand – results in the end proved better than fair words. While I was leading the horse around, Harold gave Kenny his instructions. He didn't seem to be saying a lot. Mr Hayes just stood there looking a bit self-conscious. He'd a right to. It was his first meeting as an owner. I hadn't seen Staff Ingham, though I knew he was around somewhere.

It was now getting near time for the horses to ride up to the start. So Ken Gethin took over from me and I was left standing there with the stable gear under my arm and a lot of anxiety in my heart when the governor came up to me looking tense and worried. 'Phil,' he said, 'it was true wasn't it what you said about St Andrew after that gallop?' 'Yes, Harold,' I said, 'I give you my word it was. Why, what's the matter?' 'Well,' he replied, 'Staff's been talking to some of the jockeys in the changing-room and it seems there's another big gamble apart from Walter Nightingall's Aristocracy, on a horse called Mannance. Staff doesn't think ours stands a chance against either of 'em.' This I'd found was the trouble with jockeys. They felt superior to a stable lad and therefore more knowledgeable. I'd have thought though that Staff would have had more sense because he'd come up the hard way. I said something like this to Harold. 'But it isn't only Staff. Stan Wootten's here. He knows St Andrew's history and he's told Staff that St Andrew's outclassed in this company.' I could see that Harold had the real jitters. It was as if he didn't want to be convinced. 'Look,' I said, 'I've never been more confident about a horse in all my life. That's God's truth and I think you know that I know what I'm talking about.' I was going on like this to boost my own morale as much as Harold's. He looked at me for a moment and then said, 'You'd better be right, Phil, because I'm going to tell you something. I've took a mortgage on me house to back this horse,' then he walked away leaving me feeling sick inside. 'Bloody hell,' I thought, 'it's all down to me, the bleeding stable rat. The man has mortgaged his house on my say so. What if the horse gets beat? Harold is already struggling, if it loses he's going to have to struggle a bloody sight harder.'

Suddenly the game didn't seem to be worth the candle. 'Well you're on your own now, son,' I said to myself, 'though you'll be a bloody sight lonelier if the horse loses.'

I made my way to where the other lads were gathered to watch the race. Why any of us bothered I don't know because you could see precious little. It was just a wooden platform half way up the fence looking down on where the horses pulled up when they'd passed the winning post and were riding up Trundle hill towards us. I looked over to the gate and the cry went up, 'They're off!' Then there was a silence. There was no commentary in those days. After a bit the bookmakers started shouting new odds as they watched through their binoculars. I started searching the field to see if I could see our colours, zingari with red and gold lines. Zingari was black. I could see nothing. I searched still harder as they came round the bend towards the winning post, still nothing. Now the horses were running in a straight line at us. The crowds in the stands started to shout and the shout went into a roar as they passed the winning post. Then the roar died down to a quiet murmur. Even as they were pulling up I didn't get a sight of this horse of ours. 'What won?' I shouted, not really wanting to be told. No one seemed to know. 'Oh Christ,' I thought and there was a bitter taste in my mouth as I walked to the top gate the unplaced horses used. I couldn't see St Andrew anywhere. Then a lad I knew called out, 'Hey, Phil, what are you waiting for? Your horse is down at the other gate.'

I ran like lightning and just as I got to the gate, Ken Gethin came trotting in. 'Hello Kenny. Where'd you finish?' I shouted. And in his friendly Brummy way he gave me the news that I so much wanted to hear, 'I won yer bloody fool.' My heart went from the soles of my boots to battering the top of my head off. Even Kenny's 'Well don't just stand there, take the bugger into the winning enclosure,' didn't bring me back to earth. I took hold of the reins and I started leading him in. If Gethin's reaction hadn't been enthusiastic, Harold and Mr Hayes made up for it. They patted away at the horse and the governor came up to me quietly, put his arm round my shoulder and said, 'Well done, Phil, you showed the lot of them. I shan't ever forget it.' I played it smooth. I could afford to now. 'Well, that's what the game's about guvner. When you've got a goodun, it hits yer like that' and I snapped my fingers. 'He'll win again many times I hope, sir.' The 'sir' slipped out, but it didn't pass unnoticed by Harold and I could see that to him it meant that I knew he'd made the grade, had passed that difficult hurdle from stable lad to trainer. He knew now that his success today would influence owners and that he could expect to collect one or two more horses to train almost straight away, for although on paper it seemed John Nightingall had got the credit, the racing set would soon know who was really responsible.

'Take him away, and look after him,' Harold said when the excitement had died down, and I did as I was told. While I was giving St Andrew the treatment – and did I look after that horse, he deserved it, he was the best friend I'd got in the world, I couldn't have done enough for him – old George Lawrence came running in, 'Bloody good show, that 'orse of yours Phil has done me a real good turn. I shan't forget him. He's seen me right for the meeting. 'ere, you can get him something special with this,' and he slipped a few notes into my hand. It was a countryman's way of showing his thanks to me. I walked out to the yard where Albert was waiting with the horsebox. He was over the moon too. 'Look Phil,' he said, 'I haven't collected yet. You wait here and box the horse while I get the money.' 'No, Albert,' I said, 'I'll walk him down to Singleton. It'll give him a chance to cool down.' It gave me the same chance as I walked through Birdless Grove as it's called, with its lovely leafy paths and overhanging trees. I stopped from time to time to let St Andrew munch at the lush grass. I reckoned that God was in his heaven smiling down on both of us.

Even on foot I beat Albert to it and I'd finished doing St Andrew over by the time he arrived. He came into the box looking flushed and excited. 'Come outside Phil, over by the box.' Then he began talking. 'Before the race, after I left you in the yard, I went straight round to the tote like you said and placed our bet. Then I thought I'd see what the bookies were showing. St Andrew opened at 15–1 and it stayed steady round about that figure until just before the off. Then the money came for it, boom, boom, boom, and it was returned 13 to 2.' 'That's fine, Albert,' I said impatiently. 'But what did he pay on the tote?' 'You'll never believe it, Phil, 'e paid 25 to 1.' It really was my day. I started laughing, I'd won £625. It was the sort of money I'd never even thought about. I was rich. 'When you've finished larking about, we'll get inside the box and have a share-out.' Albert's remark brought me to my senses.

I'll never forget that share-out. Albert had got a new leather coat on and each time he put his hands into the pockets it squeaked. He kept pulling notes out in handfuls and dropping them on the straw, and there we sat like a couple of bank robbers counting the loot. Eventually it ran out. 'That's all the money, Phil,' Albert said. 'It's not all that's due to me,' I said a bit suspiciously. He laughed. 'No, but that's all they gave me in cash. The rest's on this,' and he fished into his pocket and with another squeak brought out a cheque. It was big, about eighteen inches long and across the top was a scroll – Race Course Betting Control Board. It was green, a pale green. I looked at the pile of cash and I looked at this cheque. I must have done this ten times, I just couldn't believe it.

Then we started to drive back, singing all the way. We hadn't gone far when it started to rain. It came down in buckets, typical Goodwood weather, but I couldn't have cared less. It was after six when we reached Epsom. Albert was all for calling in for a drink to celebrate, but I wanted to get St Andrew bedded down for the night, so we went straight to John Nightingall's yard. We drew up outside and started to unfasten the back of the horse box when Albert called, 'Look out, Phil, we seem to have a reception committee.' I glanced up and there coming towards us were John and Walter Nightingall and judging by the expressions on their faces we weren't going to get the heroes' welcome. 'You can put that flap back and piss off. That horse isn't coming back here, not after what you and Harold have done to me,' Walter bellowed at us. 'What do you mean sir?' I said, all innocent. 'You know bloody well what I mean, you and that bastard Harold carted me in that gallop. Couple of bloody tricksters, that's what you are and you've cost me a bleeding fortune today. For two pins I'd knock your block off, you wily little sod, and do the same to Harold when I see him.' 'I'm sure I dunno what you're talking about, sir,' I said as haughtily as I could muster. During Walter's outburst, Holy John had stood there like St Peter at the Pearly Gates. Finally he spoke. 'Fuck off, Welsh,' he said. I knew now for certain there was no chance of St Andrew having a bed there for the night, or ever again for that matter.

'What the hell do we do,' Albert asked when we'd got back in the box. 'I'll phone the guvner,' I said. So we drove to the nearest kiosk. He wasn't in, and it didn't need any supernatural powers to guess that he was celebrating his good fortune. Then I had a brain wave. I had an old pal, Wally Green, who looked after the horses for John Coleman. He was a partner in one of Epsom's oldest firms of veterinary surgeons. He had a number of boxes for sick horses. Albert and I drove round to see him. I told him the mess we were in; the first thing he wanted to know was why we had been barred from John's yard. I told him the story and he didn't like the sound of it. 'The guvner's not going to like it either. Walter's a good customer of ours, but seeing you're in a hole, Phil, I'll let you have a box for the night and we can sort things out in the morning.' That was good enough for me, though it wasn't for St Andrew. It was a rough old place, shaped in a kind of triangle, not what the horse was used to, and certainly not the sort of lodging place for a king to spend the night in. He wasn't too keen about going into it either, half scared he was, but by the time I'd done it over he seemed more contented. 'We'll sort something different out for you tomorrow,' I promised him as I left.

I thought about going home and writing a note to Harold, but I decided against it. I'd get up early in the morning and go and see him. There was now one person whom I wanted to tell my good tidings to, and that was Cath. The money I'd won meant that we could get married. Of course, I hadn't told her anything about my gamble, she'd have been dead against it, so for that matter would any woman. Still, she wouldn't mind now that I'd won. She'd think how clever I'd been. It was getting late, but she worked nights and would be home by now. I made my way round and knocked at her door. I was glad she opened it, I didn't want to explain why I was there to her mum and dad first. 'Hallo, Phil,' she said 'what're you doing round here at this time of night?' I suppose in my excitement I didn't explain what had happened very well, I just gabbled away at her, then pulled out the money and the cheque. 'Don't you see, we can get married now,' I said. She looked first at the money, then at the cheque, then the tears started. 'Oh Phil,' she cried, 'what've you done?' I saw her eyes close and I put out an arm quick and caught her as she sparked straight out. Just at that moment the living-room door opened and her mum and dad came into the hall. 'What've

Harold Wallington, the Epsom trainer, on his hack Rufus, 1968.

Walter Nightingall's string being exercised on the Downs, 1950.

Walter Nightingall discussing the morning's training programme
on Epsom Downs with Stan Pullen.

Harold Wallington's Faultless Speech wins Royal Hunt Cup at
Ascot, 1959, ridden by Geoff Lewis.

Mrs Wallington pats her husband's
horse after his win in the Royal
Hunt Cup. Author holds horse
extreme right.

Mon Plaisir, ridden by Geoff
Lewis, winning the Newbury
Spring Cup, 1970.

Harold Wallington's Hasty Cloud in the stable yard at Epsom,
1964, ridden by Jock Wilson and held by the author, after winning
the Cambridgeshire.

you been doing to our Cathy?' her mum shouted as she grabbed her out of my arms. I opened my mouth to explain but it was too late. 'Get out of this house and don't come back, you dirty little stable rat, you.' I backed through the door just as Cath's dad shut it in my face.

Not exactly the sort of ending I'd hoped for what had seemed to me a few hours ago to be my perfect day.

7

Harold Wallington, trainer – Starting a stable from scratch –
Jack Reardan's revenge – St Andrew builds more than his own
reputation – A striking disaster – Hill Crest Stables – The course
of true love – Marriage: taking a gamble to take a gamble –
Undertones of war – Shut down

'After you leave me, you'll be able to do anything,' Herbert
Smythe had boasted when I joined him, and in some ways he was
right. There was little in the way of jobs around the house and
garden that I couldn't put a useful hand to, and it served me well
over the years. I also thought I knew a deal about horses, but
when I look back on those years, I realize how little I really knew,
and as I became more experienced, and was given more responsibility, I began to understand how much I'd still to learn, until
towards the end of my time in stables I was forced to the conclusion that if I lived to be a hundred horses would still surprise
me.

What it was that kept me walking away from Herbert's yard
when every instinct was telling me to turn back, I shall never
know. One thing is certain, I've never had any long-term cause to
regret what I did. My first reaction was one of hurt that Herbert
made no move to get me back. I felt then, and I still do today, that
we had had a special relationship. I'd served him loyally and
well, done all that was ever asked of me without moaning or
shirking. I'd got on well with his sons and Mrs Smythe and I
believed I'd come closer to them as a family than I was to my
own. Yet he'd allowed an association of nine years to go for
nothing over a piddling row about me joining the union. But as I
thought deeper, I came to believe that it was this special relationship that was the root of his attitude. He looked on himself
as a father figure, and by joining the union it seemed to him as if

I'd taken against him – spat in his face. Today unions are not popular with employers, but at that time in any ordinary business they were the enemy. Racing was run and controlled almost exclusively by ex-army officers, and with the same rigid discipline of service life, so even to consider taking action against the system was the equivalent to mutiny. When I got my card I hadn't realized this. I was no banner carrier, to me it had seemed like joining a club and in those terms it made a lot of sense, after all trainers met together to talk business, so why shouldn't stable lads? I'd no thought of wanting to walk out on my horses, I never have and I never could, nor have I ever felt hard done by. My track record speaks for itself. I only worked for two governors in nearly forty years. I've never been a radical, indeed, as this book is witness, I haven't even welcomed changes. I'm of the Herbert Smythe school, 'That's the way it was in my day, and that's the way it ought to be now.'

Looking back, I don't believe my life would have been any different had I stayed with him. When I'd gone into racing, it had been with the hope that one day I'd make a jockey. I still cherish the dream that had Lady Luck smiled on me I'd have made it. All told I suppose Herbert gave me some sixty rides, and later I had more than that with Harold Wallington, but they were either on horses being given outings or those with little chance. Herbert had two sons of around my age as apprentices, and not unnaturally he gave them the greater opportunities. I'm not complaining. As a father I'd have done the same, and they proved worthy of his confidence in them. In gambling stables, trainers can't afford to take chances. Nevertheless, if I'd shown exceptional promise and ability, there is no doubt it would have been recognized.

My career developed so gradually that by the time it became obvious that I would never make the grade as a rider, I felt neither disappointment nor regret. My interest in and love for horses was enough for me, and would be for the rest of my life.

It was of course inevitable that Herbert and I would meet from time to time. For the first few weeks after I left him I tried to avoid any such encounter. Eventually I got used to just not being there as far as he was concerned. When about a year later our paths crossed, I was riding St Andrew out at the time, it suddenly seemed as if no harsh words had ever passed between us. ' 'allo,

Philup. You've got a goodun there, and they tell me most of it's down to you.' Then with a twinkle he said, 'Shows what being brought up by a good guvner can do for you, eh?' and he rode off. From then on we were back on terms again. I reckon we both knew we'd made mugs of ourselves.

The circumstances under which I'd joined forces with Harold Wallington made for a different kind of relationship. At the beginning I'd done him a good turn in agreeing to look after St Andrew. His success was, as Herbert had put it, down to me. I had also proved to be trustworthy and I was the sort of lad he needed to help him through the difficult period of building a stable of horses. I was young enough to take orders and not to make demands, yet sufficiently experienced and hard-working to get the best out of any animal. We also spoke the same language. He'd been born and bred in Harpole, a small Northamptonshire village in the great hunting country. He had served some time with a man called Bletsoe up north, and later in Berkshire with Teddy Martin, before joining M. D. Blair at Ewhurst and Peaslake in Surrey.

Harold was always a man with a purpose and once he'd made up his mind to do a thing, he saw it through to the end, and as his enthusiasm for an idea was catching, he was able to take his staff with him. He wasn't as hard a man as Herbert Smythe, his manner was easier, and he was on terms with everyone who worked for him. He had to be. After the war labour was short. Many of the stable lads who'd gone into the forces didn't return to racing, they'd either put on too much weight or found other jobs that were easier and paid more. They didn't want the disciplined life of a stable, which was as strict and demanding as anything they'd experienced during the war, they weren't going to exchange one sergeant-major for another. Another factor in Harold's favour was that success didn't go to his head. Harold developed a greater authority, but he didn't go in for flash cars, women or the high life. I think, like me, he'd seen only too often what it had done to others on their way up.

His major fault was that he was over-secretive, he kept too much to himself, which at times made my life difficult and irksome. He was the same with his son, young Harold, whom he'd looked after well, putting him through veterinary college, and finally taking him on as assistant trainer. Having done this, it

132

was to be expected that he'd share his knowledge, his hopes and ambitions with the boy. He didn't. His son was continually coming to me for information, and as often as not we'd both of us have to guess what his father's intentions were. I kept telling Harold that he wasn't being fair to either of us. At the time he'd agree, and would mend his ways for a few days, but then he'd be back to square one and so would the rest of us. Yet above all Harold was a fair man, giving praise where it was due. It was this, and the fact that I grew up with his stable, that made me stay with him for the rest of my racing career.

The morning after St Andrew's success, I woke up still in a bit of a daze, and it wasn't until I'd opened the drawer where I'd put my money and the cheque and handled them again that I was able to convince myself it hadn't all been a dream. Then I realized there was a deal of sorting out to be done both in my work and private life. The first thing was to meet Harold and for us to find somewhere for St Andrew to be stabled. The governor forestalled me. He'd been round early to John Nightingall's yard and had been given the same treatment that I'd had the night before. He came into Auntie's as I was eating breakfast, 'Where the hell's the horse, Phil?' I gave him the whole rigmarole. As we walked up to Wally Green's place he did some quick thinking, and by the time I'd done St Andrew over, he'd made arrangements to rent a yard owned by Mr Boxall, an estate agent and amateur rider. He owned Sandown Lodge where there were two yards, one with wooden boxes and the other brick-built. We took over the wooden ones. We were now in business, all we needed was another eleven horses to fill them.

In my experience there are several ways by which someone without money, family connections or influence can become a successful trainer. The first is to show results through a horse, as we did with St Andrew, and of course in the process to put a certain amount of money into the kitty. Then, as Harold did, it is necessary to get a few grateful owners from the past who are prepared to follow you when you leave the previous stable. There is also the attraction that horses are likely to receive more attention and better treatment from a small man with a reputation to make who also at the beginning can't charge the full amount, his fees must grow with his reputation. Finally, as in Harold's case, there was the knowledge that he was prepared to bend the rules a bit. News travels fast in racing, and people soon learned of the gamble we'd pulled off at Goodwood which outwitted not only Walter Nightingall's stable, but also that of the trainer, Jack Reardon, whose horse Mannance had been placed second.

Jack's was a real gambling stable, six winners a year was all he wanted. I was able to hear first-hand what St Andrew's winning had meant to him, for shortly after the meeting I was exercising the horse, giving him an easy time on the sand track, when Reardon came up alongside. I gave him a friendly 'Mornin', sir', but got no acknowledgement. Inwardly I cursed him for an ignorant swine, and waited for him to move on. He didn't, he just kept staring down at my horse. Eventually he spoke. 'Is that St Andrew?' I nodded. 'I'd like to shoot the bastard.' 'Now why would you like to do that, he's done you no harm,' I said innocently, though I knew something of his reason. 'Do you know,' he said, 'when he beat us at Goodwood I had four thousand quid of me own money on Mannance and your guv'ner knew it.' There was nothing I could say, though I could now understand his behaviour, even if what he said was an exaggeration. When I repeated our conversation later, I had it confirmed, for just as bookies have their underground sources of information, so do trainers and it was being bandied around that Reardon would have had even more money on, but the bookies just weren't taking it.

The first horse to follow St Andrew into our stable was a jumper, Good Sport, which was more than the owner was called when he bought it cheap after it had won a seller in the West Country, taking both the owner and trainer unawares when they'd wanted to keep it. It created a deal of bad feeling, some of which brushed off on to Harold. Still the horse performed well, which was more than compensation for the rough words. He was also a good lead horse for St Andrew on exercise and gallops. Our third was another jumper, Rao Sahib. He won a couple of races for us at small meetings and though the prize money was poor, the return from the bookmakers was good. With these horses we managed in a few months to get our fair share of winners.

This success attracted a string of three from a Mr Cohen, again all of them jumpers, and we did well with these. The trouble with Jewish owners is that while they respect their own Sabbath of a Saturday, they have scant regard for the Christian and his Sunday. In stables, Sundays are recognised as easy days, but for Mr Cohen and other Jewish owners it was a holiday and what better way of spending it than taking a look at their horses. This meant that they had to be especially well groomed and that the trainer, head lad and stable lad were there to welcome owners and their guests. The governor wasn't particularly worried, he didn't have the dirty work to do and there was always the chance that he might persuade an owner to take on another animal, or if he brought friends with him, that one of them could be talked into owning a horse. It was as well there was some consolation for the lads, for the Jewish fraternity are very generous, free with their money, so there was almost always something on the end of it, and this didn't come just from the owner, but from his pals. Then, since Jews are great family men, any stable lad worth his salt always had a few lumps of sugar in his pocket so that their children could feed these to the horses. This brought its reward. Jews are also funny punters. A good win sends them wild with delight, but if they lose, they moan and groan and swear they'll never gamble again. The next day, when you see them placing a large bet, you remind them of their vows; 'Yes, but it was yesterday I said that' they say with a grin.

Soon the stable work was getting far too much for the governor and me to manage on our own. We were lucky to get the part-time services of a trained lad, Ray Groombridge, who'd recently joined Walter Nightingall, ridden a couple of winners for him, and then to his astonishment had been ignored. In his disappointment he decided to give the game up, but while he was starting a business as a window cleaner he was happy to earn a few bob on the side. Apart from his stable work, Harold and I had reason to be grateful to Ray, for the governor decided it was time he had a car. He didn't go mad, he bought an Austin 7 Ruby saloon that looked as if it travelled on pram wheels. When it was delivered to the yard, all he could do was gaze at it. I was no help, but Ray knew how to drive, so Harold and I took it in turns going round the paddock with him. Ray would sit by us, telling us what to do, then he'd make us slow down, open the passenger door and bale out. 'You're on your own now, just put it into a canter,' and he'd shout instructions at us like old Herbert did when he was teaching anyone to ride. It may not have been the orthodox way to learn, but it worked. Harold became an excellent driver, never had a scratch on any of his cars. As for me, it probably saved me a lot of foot-slogging when I joined the army.

It was early in 1938 that Harold had his first setback, and Jack Reardon got his revenge. Knowing what a horse we had with St Andrew, Harold persuaded a pal of his, Mr Mansell, a local contractor, to buy Mannance from Reardon. As I've said, he had come in second to us at Goodwood, run a fine race, and on the face of it he seemed a good buy. We knew, though, there must be a reason for Jack wanting to off-load him, after all we were neither of us greenhorns, and we saw that he'd got a bit of a leg, that his tendon was dodgy and showed signs of strain. However, the governor was convinced that between us we could put it right. 'We showed them with St Andrew, Phil, I'm certain we could do it with this one.' I went along with him. After all, we'd only got to have it off with him once or twice for us to see more than our money back. We gave the horse the full treatment, blistered him, got him fit and going like a bomb. We entered him in a race at Leicester, and he was the nearest thing to a certainty that I'd ever known apart from St Andrew. So before the race the governor and I moved near to the winning gate ready to lead him in.

Harold had engaged Jackie Sirett as rider, a well-known lightweight jockey at that time, and Mannance was only carrying seven stone-ten. I heard the governor give him his instructions. 'Now Jack, keep him covered up, then about a furlong and a half from home, bring him to the front and you'll win' – short but very much to the point. The moment the tape went up, Harold and I both knew that our horse was beaten. Mannance went away fast, was in front by the first furlong, made every inch of the running and was second by a neck, and all because Jackie had ignored what he had been told. His excuse was that the animal had pulled too strongly for him, and that knowing he had a dodgy leg he didn't want to pull him in case he went lame. To give him his due, he was right about that, for when a horse has an 'if', it's better to let him use his own stride for by restraining him you risk altering his balance and putting extra strain on his legs. Still, this excuse didn't satisfy the governor. 'He'd have won on three legs if only you'd done as I said,' he remarked bitterly. As it was, the horse's leg did break down again and Harold was so disappointed that he sold him for a song. I don't think Jack Reardon had a bet on him that time for he was seen smirking around Epsom for days, and boasting about having had his revenge.

The year 1938 had started well for us. St Andrew had won the Brighton Spring Cup, a big race in the South with good prize money and a lot of prestige. A certain amount of the success was put down to me, and with Epsom still very much a racing town, I'd be stopped in the street with, 'How's that horse of your's going, Phil? Bloody good animal that. He hasn't half altered since you've been looking after him.' I know the old saying 'fine words don't butter no parsnips', but a little praise and recognition were music to my ears. It was some compensation for the time and trouble I had to use on St Andrew, for he was still difficult and troublesome. He was like a spoiled child. He had to be nursed, given his own way much of the time. He would only respond to kindness and this was difficult to give when he was being awkward and stubborn.

Harold and I had come to an agreement that no one was to have anything to do with St Andrew except myself. Not even the governor ever rode the horse, so we were both put back on our heels when Staff Ingham arrived at the stables one morning and asked to ride him out. Naturally he assumed he had the right since he was part owner. It was a decision for the governor to make so I kept out of it. Later Harold told me that if only I had protested, he'd have said no, but as it was he gave way. Although I knew Staff was a first-class jockey, I had a feeling of foreboding. When they got to the gallop, I saw some horses approaching, and as he always did when this happened, St Andrew stopped in his tracks. He stood there transfixed with not a muscle in his body moving. 'Let him be,' I shouted to Staff, 'Wait for them to pass, then he'll go with you.' Staff took no notice. 'I'm not standing for this lark. He's got to know what he's here to do,' and he raised his stick to strike him on the shoulder. The horse sensed what he was doing and in his surprise turned and lowered his head, so that as the stick came down it hit him in the eye. St Andrew went berserk, threw Staff, and might have jumped on him if I hadn't caught him in time – not that I would have cared at that moment if he had killed him. When I'd quietened the horse down a bit and was able to look at his eye, I went sick inside, it was scarlet and bleeding.

By now Harold had arrived. He'd seen what had happened,

and after he'd had a quick look at the horse, he waded into Staff, calling him every name in the book. It wasn't surprising, it looked as if Harold had lost the jewel in his crown. My concern was for the horse. With some difficulty I was able to lead him back to the stable. The governor and Staff meantime had got on some sort of terms again and Harold phoned the vet, Mr Bowen-Jones. He came straightaway, but his report did little to cheer us up. 'It'll be touch and go whether he loses the sight of that eye or not!'

St Andrew now had to be kept in the dark. We fitted him with a night cap, a piece of harness which goes over the head, with two holes for the eyes and two for the ears. It's used to keep the head dry in the rain and warm in the winter. I was instructed to get a conical patch made to fit over the damaged eye and was also given a prescription for eye drops. I went to a saddler in Epsom, not surprisingly known as Deafy Oxley for he was both deaf and dumb. In a matter of seconds he'd picked up a piece of basil leather, a sort of grained hide, thrown it into a bowl of water, hammered and stretched it into a dome shape, trimmed and put in into the eye-piece of the night cap and stitched it into place while it was still wet. He then padded it with paper, conveyed to me that I was to leave it there all night while it dried, but that the next day I could exercise the horse with him wearing it. He then charged me a shilling for his troubles.

The following day I began riding out with St Andrew. It was, as I knew it would be, terrifying. To begin with, he was angry and resentful: he remembered what had happened the day before. Gradually I got him to go, but the slightest movement on his blind side made him edgy and uncertain. He imagined obstacles and started propping and copping, half jumping over what he thought he saw. Directly he heard another horse he'd stop and it was the devil's own job getting him to move again. At other times he'd go hard and I'd be shit-scared that he would crash into something. I had to do the steering and all the time I was wondering if he'd got his trust and confidence back, or whether he'd return to his bad habits or lose his form altogether. Then, when it seemed he was going better, getting back to his old self, it became almost worse for me, for I knew that one slip up and he'd be back to square one. I wasn't finished with him either when I got him safely into stables. There were the eye drops to be put in three times a day. To say that this was difficult would be a gross understatement – as I got crafty so did St Andrew and I often ended up on the box floor.

It was about a couple of weeks before the vet was able to pronounce that the eye would be all right, and his sight not impaired. I don't think I've ever worked so long and so unstintingly. I was literally willing that animal back into condition. I wasn't alone. Both the governor and Staff Ingham were constant visitors. Staff would stay behind after Harold had left. He was all apologies and tried to show it by offering to do any menial task. It was pathetic in a way to see a first-class jockey turned stable lad again. He wanted to show me that not only had he learned his lesson, but he was going to pay for it. It was the measure of a man who was later to become one of our leading trainers and the best of his time with middle-distance horses and two-year-olds.

As a result of his injury, we had to withdraw St Andrew from the next Brighton meeting where he'd been entered for the Balcombe Stakes. Now his target was the Brighton Summer Cup. There were more anxious moments when we were able to remove the eye patch. We wondered if he'd get back to thinking about the job in hand or whether his thoughts would be to keep himself out of trouble. Our fears were short-lived, I could feel the old spirit surge back into him, he was ready to prove himself again, and he did. He won the Summer Cup. breaking the course record, then went to Redcar and broke another there, and ended up a brilliant season by winning the Brighton Autumn Cup. He also won the Durdens Handicap at Epsom and was second by a neck to a horse called Red Devil, who was later third in the Derby, at a race at Newmarket. Now of course we were entering him for the prestige of winning, not for the gambles, though Harold made plenty backing him, for he never started at a lower price than 11–8. The governor's reputation as a trainer was well and truly made. We moved to Hill Crest Stables which had once been the property of George Barclay, the husband of Kate Carney, the famous music hall artist, who'd had her horses trained there. They weren't large premises, Harold's ambitions didn't stretch so far, nor was he in too much of a hurry. He thought he had plenty of time, but like a lot of other people he reckoned without the war.

Despite being busy at the stables, I was still able to find time to continue my courting. There's a saying, 'The course of true love never did run smooth', and our early years of romance were no exception. Both Mr and Mrs Allen were formidable people. He was a Scotsman who'd emigrated to Canada, and during the war he'd returned to England as a sergeant major in the Canadian Scottish. I understand that the Canadian troops didn't take easily to the normal army discipline; to be even an ordinary N.C.O. you had to be hard and tough, so to be a sergeant major you had to be a Cassius Clay with a tongue of a rattle snake and a heart of flint. Now I don't want to be hard on the man, who was to become my father-in-law, but that's how he must have been before he met Cath's mum, and the fact that she tamed him is all that needs to be said about her. He could still occasionally revert to type, as I was to find out. After the war he got a job as a male nurse at the Manor Asylum and later rose to be supervisor there. He was also a big noise in the Epsom British Legion. Cath and I had been going out together for a long time before I met either of them, which I think was probably as well since our relationship by then had become strong enough to withstand their immediate opposition.

At that time courtship was different, at any rate in my class. Marriages were made to last and family unity played a large part in this. So the acceptance by parents was of great importance. Once I thought that my intentions towards Cath were serious, I decided to put her to the test. Auntie Kildare provided me with the opportunity. Her nephew Manch Taylor had signed a contract to ride in India during the winter, and she decided to give a party to celebrate. I asked if I could bring Cath along. When I saw the glint in her eye as she said, 'By all means, Phil. I shall look forward to meeting her,' I was not too sure I was doing the right thing. She could be forthright to the point of rudeness, and was as likely to say 'Who the bloody hell have you got there?' in Cath's hearing, as to welcome her into the house. As things turned out Cath was a success. She entered into the spirit of the party and made herself pleasant to Ma Kildare. It turned out that Auntie had known Cath's mother, they were about the same age, and had been to the same socials and dances when they were single. 'A most delightful girl, your mum,' had been her verdict. I was no end pleased about this, I could see that if Auntie and Mrs Allen had been pals, it would make the going easier for me. I had the smile taken off my face the next time I saw Cath. 'I told mum what Mrs Kildare had said about her. She remembers her well, a right cow she says she was, after all the men when she was young, she even tried to get dad away from her.' I could just hear her mum saying it, and insinuating that since I was living with Auntie I was almost certainly tarred with the same brush.

I now decided to try a different ploy. I'd met Cath's grand-mother once; she'd been staying with her when her parents were away and I'd been invited into her home. We'd got on well, she'd been in service in Epsom and had been around with the racing crowd and understood them. Unfortunately she'd also married into the army, a regular soldier with a regimental manner, who seemed to have a nasty smell under his nose when I was around. However, I decided to work on Gran. I made myself useful and ended up painting and decorating the house. At first her old man didn't care for this – I think he thought it reflected on him – but when he saw the results, his attitude changed and we got on terms. This way things seemed to be proceeding quite happily. Cath's parents warmed towards me when they saw the job I'd done, and though we still hadn't enough money to get married on, prospects didn't look too bad. Then I walked out on Herbert, and everything collapsed around me like a pack of cards.

When Cath's parents heard about the union, it was the end. Enough of the Canadian way of life had brushed off on Mr Allen for him to consider unions the work of the devil, so in his eyes I became Satan's right-hand man. Fortunately Cath stood by me, though she was under considerable strain. St Andrew, seemed to have changed the situation. To give Mr and Mrs Allen their due, it wasn't just the money I'd made, they knew that I'd now a fair reputation in the town as a good stableman. Nevertheless, I noticed that after a couple of weeks when the excitement had died down, their attitude towards me was cooling, so I decided to get in quick while I still had some credit left. I first approached Mrs Allen. Her response was not encouraging. 'You'll have to ask Cath's dad,' she said, but the way she said it, she obviously didn't rate my chances better than around 20–1. 'When will he be in?' I asked. 'Well, he's working late shift tonight and then going on to the Legion. You can wait up for him if you like, though Cath and I will be going to bed.' I decided to sit it out.

I settled down in an easy chair with a newspaper. It was a

warm summer evening, and I must have got drowsy and fallen asleep. I woke up as the door opened. It was now dark. It took me a second two to remember where I was. That was too long. I must have rustled the paper and startled Mr Allen, for suddenly I was grasped round the waist, held in a half-Nelson and propelled down the corridor to the front door. I tried making a few noises so that he would recognize me before he decided to knock me out cold. I was lucky, he peered into my face. 'Oh, it's you,' he said, sounding disappointed. 'What the bloody hell are you doing here at this time of night?' For a split second I thought of telling him, then quickly changed my mind. This was no time to be asking for his daughter's hand in marriage. I just gawped at him. 'Oh bugger off home you stupid sod,' he said, flinging me from him. 'We'll sort this out tomorrow.' So for the second time I left the house with my tail between my legs.

All through stable work next day I was puzzling how I was going to play it with Mr Allen when we met, and wondering what Cath was going to say. I'd made no plan when I went to see her at the cinema that night and my heart was down in my boots. She showed me to a seat, I could tell something was up, she seemed all excitement. She sat next to me and I waited to hear what she had to say. It came out like a hiss from a steam engine,' Isn't it wonderful Phil, we can get engaged.' My astonished 'What! ' came out like a bullet from a gun, and there were shush's all over the cinema. It appeared that I'd misjudged her dad, he had a sense of humour after all and when he was told why I'd been sitting up waiting for him, fell about laughing. The important thing though was that he gave his consent. When I went home with Cath that night, he took one look at me and starting guffawing all over again. Apparently he drank out on the story for weeks so I got some strange looks from around the town. It didn't worry me for Cath and I could now make plans for our wedding. We rented a flat and furnished it. I could now introduce both sets of parents. I hadn't dared to while the Allens were if-ing and but-ing, neither mum nor dad would have taken kindly to any criticism of their son. In fact they both got on well together, and we were eventually given a great send-off. Even Mrs Allen and Auntie behaved like bosom pals. It was a pity that the war had to interrupt our early happiness.

The year 1939 began well for our stables. St Andrew again

won the Brighton Spring Cup and all our boxes were now full. We also had high hopes that St Andrew would do well at stud. I suppose it was natural that the sound of war drums would first be heard in the racing world with so many military men in control, and many others as owners, trainers or amateur riders. They knew that a war would mean at the best that the number of meetings would shrink, that many courses would be taken over by the army, that manpower and feed would be in short supply, so that a number of horses would have to be taken out of training, and that at the worst racing could be stopped altogether. They began making plans accordingly, and their actions were catching. Others, myself and Harold included, were more optimistic. We had to be, success and happiness had become part of our way of life, we didn't want to believe that it would be snatched from us. So the declaration of war came as a shock. Still, like many others, there was nothing we could do, except wait and see what happened. I think the thing that really brought it home to me was when I collected my gas mask. It was all very well for humans, but what about my poor bloody horses, had I just got to stand by and watch them suffocate?

Racing stopped, of course, as did all public entertainment where crowds might assemble. Then came the period of the phoney war, but still racing didn't start up again. Some of us thought it should have, but we had to wait for the authorities to approve and organize it. I continued looking after St Andrew, though Harold had decided we should sell him to stud. There wasn't a market here, of course: we had a good offer from America, but finally he was bought by a stables in the Argentine. There was, however, his passage to be arranged, and that didn't prove easy. Before Harold was able to negotiate it, I got my call-up papers. That put the cat among Harold's pigeons, as I was the only one to have looked after St Andrew. He wanted me to apply for a postponement. I did, but the powers that be quite rightly decided that there were more important things for me to do than looking after horses. I'm glad to say, though, that for much of the war the reins were never far from my hands.

8

Infantry training in Dorset – Groom and batman – Master in my own little world – A day at Salisbury Races – Getting away with murder – In Algiers with the First Army – Italy and changing mounts: tanks for horses – Changing mounts again: mules for tanks – Armistice; sorting out the captured blood-stock – Race meetings: entertainments for the troops – How to make a fortune by punting – It's harder to give money away than to make it – Returning home

Anyone who said that the army put square pegs into round holes, wanted his head examined. On second thoughts, that's not quite true. At the start people may have been put into jobs they weren't suited to, but for anyone using his head, there was always the chance to find a suitable billet. By that I don't mean that you could dodge the column and keep out of the line of fire. The war was like racing in that respect, the more you tried to keep out of trouble, the more likely you were to run into it.

These were not my thoughts when I got my call-up papers, with instructions to report to the Bridging Camp, Wyke Regis, near Chickerell, Dorset, on 1 July 1940. I was to become a member of the Dorset Regiment. My first reaction on receiving the posting was that the clerk had got it wrong, that if I was going to a bridging camp I must be joining the Royal Engineers. I didn't fancy building bridges for the rest of the war. 'Just my luck,' I said to my already tearful Cath, 'I'll be mucking about in the water, and I can't swim a bleedin' stroke.' I was sent a rail warrant to Weymouth. When I got there, it was the usual thing, a sergeant and four junior N.C.O.s walking the platform, all shouting at once at blokes who were jumping around and falling over each other like a flock of frightened sheep. Eventually we got the message that we had to get into the lorries that were waiting outside to take us to our destination.

What a lovely setting it was, right out in the wilds, nestling in a green sward which led down to the sea. Just the place for a week's summer holiday. The trouble was it was covered in bell tents and marquees, we were going to be there for at least a couple of months, and it was certainly going to be no holiday. We were detailed off, eight to a tent, drew ground sheets and a couple of blankets, were issued with uniforms, fed with food cooked by someone who must have taken an instant dislike to us, and eventually went to bed on a mattress of chalk and Portland stone.

The next morning we had a friendly welcoming talk from our company commander, Captain Grayson, which he ended by telling us that if we had any problems we should go and see him about them. It was as if we'd only got to knock on his door and he'd welcome us with open arms. In fact it was more difficult than it would have been to arrange an audience with the Pope. This address was followed by an equally amiable get-together with our C-platoon sergeant, a bloke with cow-like eyes who spoke with a soft country brogue, and welcomed us as as nice and intelligent-looking bunch as he'd ever seen – and spent the next weeks in a state of hysteria proving himself a bloody liar. We were then issued with picks and shovels and told to dig slit trenches outside our tents. We were the first intake at that camp since the last war. It had been used in peace time as an army training camp, hence the name.

Though we had it rough over the next few weeks, I reckon I was one of the lucky ones. My old life fitted me for this new one. When our nine weeks' preliminary training was over, it was announced that our company was to become part of the new 8th Battalion Dorset Regiment. We were also told that we would be on coastal defence. I didn't fancy the same daily routine only interrupted by guard duty. I could drive, and I liked the idea of being behind a wheel. While I was making a few inquiries from the clerk outside company office, Captain Grayson saw me. 'Ah, Welsh, just the man I want to see. Come on in.' I didn't like his affable tone. In my limited military experience when you were spoken to like that there was generally some awful chore at the end of it. 'Now Welsh,' he continued when we got inside, 'I understand that in peace time you were a jockey.' That's what

I'd put down on my form, I thought it sounded better than stable lad. 'Yes, that's right, sir,' I said. 'Does that mean you know anything about grooming or looking after horses?' That was an easy one to answer, but I played it cautiously. 'I know a bit, sir.' 'Oh, that's good because Major Warrell, commanding D Company, has a horse at a farm at company HQ near Lyme Regis, and he's stumped for someone to look after it. Would you be interested?' 'I'd like to meet Major Warrell, and have a look at the horse, sir,' I said, so expressing interest and allowing myself a bolt hole. 'Good man, I'll arrange it,' the Captain said as if the matter was settled.

The more I thought about it the more I liked the idea, but I decided first to try and get myself over to D Company area and find out more about this Major Warrell. He didn't sound too promising. 'Hard bastard', 'strict disciplinarian', 'one of the old school tie,' then I remembered that these comments were given by chaps just out of civvy street and with no knowledge of the racing scene. It fitted many I'd known or worked for, so when I met him a couple of days later, although he conformed to everything that had been said about him, I nearly accepted the job straightaway – then I thought I'd better ask about any other duties. 'Well there's looking after me as batman, cleaning my boots and Sam Browne and polishing my buttons.' 'So I've got two lots of harness to see to,' I said. He thought this funny. 'Something like that I suppose. Then there's waiting in the officer's mess.' That worried me. 'I've never done that sort of thing before.' He scoffed my fears away. 'Well, sir, supposing I take the job on a week's trial, on both sides that is.' 'That's fine, Welsh. Now you go and have a word with the mess corporal and he'll put you in the picture.' This I did. I was worried about waiting at the table, I told him I was used to feeding animals not officers. His 'You won't notice the difference,' wasn't particularly helpful.

When I reported for duty the following day at the company office, the sergeant major was there on his own. 'So you're another bugger dodging the column are you, Welsh? We don't like skivers in this company. We'll have to see you don't get away with too much, won't we?' I didn't feel called upon to answer. I settled in quite happily, and then reading company orders, I saw I was down for guard duty the following day. Start as you mean to go on. I had a word with the major after lunch. 'I'm afraid I shall have to pack the job in at the end of the week, sir,' I said. He didn't like it. 'Why, Welsh, I thought you and I were getting on well together?' 'Oh, it's nothing personal, sir, it's just that I've been put on guard duty tomorrow.' 'Well, strictly speaking, Welsh, we're all of us soldiers first you know.' 'Well, I'll have to stop being a batman and a groom and just be a soldier sir, there aren't enough hours in the day otherwise.' His 'I'll see what I can do about it,' meant that I had won the day. It couldn't have been that easy for him, for the sergeant major sent for me. He was raging.

I left company office with the comfortable feeling of being master in my own small world at last. From that moment onwards the major and I got on fine. For what it was, his horse was 'a goodun' and with the constant attention and exercise I gave him, he'd never had it so good. I built some fences in a field nearby, and gave the major a few tips about riding and caring for an animal; he was a willing pupil and so a different relationship built up between us than was usual between officers and other ranks.

I suppose what really cemented my relationship with the major was a day at the races. The battalion had been sent on special training with the gunners and tanks to Tidworth Pennings camp. Salisbury was the town nearby and the course there had been zoned for racing. The meeting was on a Saturday, and as there was no training on that day, I put in for a pass through the usual channels to go to Salisbury. Without bothering to show my request to the major, the sergeant major had me in front of him and delivered a broad-side attack. 'Didn't I know there was a war on,' and accused me of shirking my way through it. I happened to mention the race-meeting in conversation with the major. He got excited about it. 'It just so happens Welsh, that I have to go to Salisbury tomorrow on duty. I shall be driving there. Perhaps you'd like to come along with me and when I've finished attending to my business, we can go along to the course together afterwards. You may meet some of your old pals, blokes in the know eh?' I didn't bother to tell him I'd been refused a pass, after all I was now going on duty, so I accepted gracefully. If he did have anything to do, it didn't take the major long. We drove up to the course in style and the driver was dismissed with instructions to meet us after the last race.

147

The major made for the Tattersalls entrance. 'I don't think it will be necessary for you to pay, sir. I think I'll be able to arrange a complimentary pass for you.' Together we went to the owners' and trainers' gate. The bloke on it was an old mate, so telling the major to wait where he was, I went scouting around for someone in authority. I hadn't gone more than a few yards when I bumped into Herbert Smythe, who was all greetings and smiles. I explained what I wanted and he was only too happy to oblige. He and Warrell got on like a house on fire, and for the first time ever, Herbert was really complimentary about me. 'So you've got Philup as your groom, well you're a very lucky man, major. He's first class at his job. I should know because I bloody well trained him. All down to me, isn't it, Philup?' So it went on.

We managed to get away at last, and I told the major I'd go round and try to find a few likely winners, and that I'd be back to mark his card. I was lucky, there were a few pals of mine around and I passed their information on to him. Two good tips I had were for the tote double. One of the horses was Irish Guardsman who won at 7–1, I can't remember the other. The tote paid out fifty odd quid for a ten bob ticket and the major had bought four of them. By the end of the meeting he'd won over £250 and the afternoon hadn't cost him a penny. Chuffed! I've never seen a man so happy, he was singing all the way back to HQ, and that night in the mess the drinks were on him, with the officers even raising a glass to me.

The major, like some other officers, was very particular about his appearance, and it had been my job early on to find someone to do his laundry. I knocked on the door in that part of the town where I thought some woman wouldn't mind earning a bob or two and I chanced on a Mrs Crabb, in Australia Road, who was willing. She was a bit class conscious about it at first. 'I'm not sure whether I can do it. I've never washed an officer's things before.' I was able to set her mind at rest. 'It's all right,' I said, 'they're almost the same as humans.' Anyway, I was able to win her a few things from the mess stores, tea and sugar and the like, and take them along to her. Knowing I was married she suggested one day that my wife might like to come down and visit me. 'I'd be only too glad to put her up,' she said. 'It's good of you, but I'm afraid it's impossible. Wives are strictly forbidden down here.' 'But who's to know she's your wife? She could easily be my sister. You think it over.'

I took her advice and the more I thought about it the better it seemed. I wrote to Cath explaining everything, she jumped at the idea, and within a week had taken up residence as a paying guest. At first I was just happy at having her there, and with us able to meet during the day, then one night, after lights out, I thought of her lying in a comfy bed, only a couple of hundred yards away, and me on a hard palliasse. I got dressed and, waiting for the patrolling guard to pass, made a dive at a hole I knew of in the hedge; I was through it like a rabbit and between the sheets with a surprised and delighted Cath. It was all too easy, and it became a habit.

One Monday morning around dawn when I was returning to my billet, I was surprised to find the whole place deserted, no one about except a few blokes who were sick and excused duty. They told me that the whole battalion had been called out at midnight on some sort of emergency, they weren't sure if it was an exercise or the real thing. 'Christ,' I thought, 'that's torn it. Now it's me for the high jump.' There was nothing I could do about it, so I just hung around the mess, hoping that they'd come back soon. They returned about midday, with everyone looking slightly knackered, which I knew wouldn't help the major's temper. He waded straight in. 'Where were you last night Welsh?' and although I expected this would be his first question, I hadn't really got an answer. 'I took your washing around to Mrs Crabb, sir, and out of the kindness of her heart she gave me some supper and accidentally I went to sleep in her armchair.' At least it was the sort of thing that had happened to me before. 'You'll have to think of something better than that, Welsh,' he said nastily. I could see what he was thinking, that I'd got a piece of stuff in the town. I was indignant. 'It's the truth, sir,' I said defiantly. 'Well, truth or not, I'll have to put you on a charge.' 'Very good, sir,' I said, deciding that now was not the time to pursue the matter further. Later that day I met the sergeant major. 'Company office for you in the morning, me lad. Told you I'd catch up with you given time. I shall look forward to seeing you.' I couldn't help thinking that if there were many other sadists like him around, we were wasting our time fighting Hitler.

I'd only one card left to play, I'd tried it before, but this time I thought it more of a trump card. I used it that evening. I told

Major Warrell that if I was put on a charge, I would have to return to ordinary soldiering. He knew what I was doing. 'You're trying to blackmail me, Welsh.' 'That's not a nice word to use, sir' I said. 'The way I look at it is that I would find it hard to work close to a man who showed no trust in me, doesn't believe my word. You take my meaning, sir? I thought that over the months we'd built up a kind of relationship between us based on trust. Now I see I was wrong.' The major knew he owed me something. 'All right Welsh, we'll forget about it this time. But if it ever happens again, I shall have no option.' I agreed with him of course. It didn't stop my frequent nightly visits, but now I arranged with a mate that if something similar occurred he would be round to Australia Road at the double to raise the alarm.

Although I was in a good position to tell what was going on, or likely to happen, there was one occasion when I was completely taken by surprise. I should have known something was up because one day out of the blue the major told me he'd decided to send his horse back home for a week or two. About a couple of days after the horse left, we were told we were taking part in a full-scale exercise which was to cover a large part of England, it was a sort of north versus south battle. I was surprised how easily we won, for it wasn't long before we found ourselves at Greenock on the Glasgow docks, and before we knew what was happening we were on board the *Stratheden*. I'd just written to Cath saying that the exercise was over and that I was due for forty-eight hours' leave the following weekend, whereas it was to be a few years before I saw her again. Eventually we were told that we were taking part in Operation Torch, the invasion of Algiers under the command of the American General Anderson, with Mark Clark GOC the whole operation.

This book, however, is not about my military exploits, which were much the same as everyone else's. I was no braver or more cowardly than others, my chief worry was not to show fear when in fact I was terrified. I knew more of what was going on than most because as well as being the major's batman I was also his runner, and had to follow him wherever he went. This had advantages and disadvantages. If he decided to do a personal reconnaissance, as he called it, to find out what the enemy was doing, I had to go with him. It was through him that I confirmed the difference between an amateur rider and a professional. The jockey, when he's riding over fences, tries to keep out of trouble; the amateur rides hard and hopes for the best. Major Warrell was a proper amateur, but he was lucky. He was good to me, though. We'd go together so far, then he'd tell me to wait for him while he went forward. Not that waiting was much fun, it was lonely and not knowing whether he'd been captured or lost on the way back didn't at times do my stomach any good. On one occasion he did meet trouble, but sorted it out. He got the Military Cross. I got the shits or squitters.

Shortly after we arrived in Algiers, we were converted into an AA regiment. With the victory in the desert, we went to Italy, and carried on the good work there. When it was found we had air supremacy, we became surplus to requirements, were split up, given aptitude tests and I found myself being trained as a tank driver. I ended up with the Warwickshire Yeomanry, and I'm happy to say that by the time it was decided to withdraw our regiment and send us back to England, I'd got through without a scratch.

A lot of our blokes were looking forward to seeing their home country again. Nothing could have pleased me better, but I reasoned it out that we'd only have a short stay, we'd be posted to France to sort out the trouble over there. I looked at it this way, Lady Luck had been on my side for nearly two years, but it was asking too much of her to expect her to stay there much longer, so when I saw a notice asking for volunteers for pack transport teams, I decided to put my name forward. It didn't look as if I'd been lucky, for I was with the regiment in a camp at Arezzo waiting to board the *Georgio*, when at three in the morning I was woken by the night sentry and told to report immediately to the orderly officer. He instructed me that a posting had come through for me to Number 4 Pack Group Horse Transport at Forli, that I was to travel on the ration truck that morning to base supply depot where I would change lorries and be taken to my destination.

The main Allied advance had been along the flat lands on either side of Italy, and the pockets of resistance in the hills had been bypassed. These were now being mopped up by the Third Indian Division. 'Mopped up' makes it sound all too straightforward, in fact it was dangerous and difficult. Supplying the troops was one of the major problems, and

151

since motorized transport could only go so far, for the remainder of the journey food, ammunition and the like had to be carried by mule transport. Since this had to be done in the dark and as the troops were constantly changing position, it wasn't an easy job. On our arrival, for there were some ten volunteers, we were put on a course of instruction. I was promoted sergeant.

We were given horses and I was taught to ride again – army style. We were supposed to use these horses to lead the mule teams, I only did once; directly it came under mortar fire the animal went berserk, whereas the mules didn't turn a hair, just got on with what they were doing. The muleteers, who came under British command, were either Indian or Cypriot, both nationalities were good at their job and fairly well disciplined. If we had any trouble with them, we docked their pay. This didn't worry them any more than it would have worried us as there was nothing to spend the money on. There were also French teams with Arabs working the mules. They were much more excitable and were continually bashing and flogging poor old Johnny Arab for the slightest mistake. The Arabs then took it out on the mules.

I hadn't done many trips before I began wondering whether I'd been so clever in leaving the tanks. Jerry was no fool and he knew that if he could stop supplies getting through, his chances of survival were that much stronger. We were guarded from attacks on our flanks but he frequently treated us to bombardments of mortar fire. Under any circumstances mortars are nasty weapons to be on the receiving end of, and they're difficult to retaliate against, but when you're going along narrow mountain paths with rocks on one side or another, they're a bloody sight nastier, for when they explode you get splinters of rocks as well as shells coming at you, and you're not there to fight back, your job is to keep moving on with the supplies.

Mules I found to be much maligned animals. 'Stubborn as a mule' is all I'd ever heard about them, and it's right, for on occasions they could be awkward, but I grew to believe it was because they are so highly intelligent. If they were overloaded, they knew it and might refuse to budge. Or sometimes, if you had to cross a stream with them, they'd stop on the bank as they'd been in water before and found it cold, and they also realized the bed of the stream made for treacherous footholds. When you got the understanding of them, there was no better animal at the job. They were sure-footed, needing less room than horses, they moved like tightrope walkers with one foot in front of another. I've seen them go along a ledge only 18 inches wide. They made excellent stretcher-bearers, they could bring back two men at a time strapped either side without causing the slightest anxiety either to us or the patients. They were brave as lions and as I've said they didn't flinch under fire, nor did they scream if they were hit. At times we wished they would for we'd arrive back at base and find them bleeding badly from their wounds which we could have attended to earlier if they'd given us a sign. We were continually on the move following the army as they cleared the hills, requisitioning farm buildings as we went and taking the farmers' fodder to feed our animals.

Eventually the armistice was signed. There were still some pockets of resistance in the hills but it was decided to let them come to terms with the situation in their own good time. Our mules were put to work on farms, but conditions were primitive so we travelled around either giving them away or loaning them out when and where they were required. We also helped the veterinary corps sort out the bloodstock horses and cattle that had been taken from occupied countries. Attempts were made to identify them and to return them to their rightful owners.

As a fringe activity, it was decided to run race meetings, using some of these horses. There was a large number of troops with little to do except sit on their hands and wait for their demob group to come up and it seemed a good way to entertain them and to keep them out of trouble. Some of the officers from the pack groups were also in on it. Stuart Murless, our adjutant, and Captain Mewburn, both peacetime trainers introduced me to Major Dennison, Ginger as he was known in the racing world. He was in the Veterinary Corps and had picked a very useful animal called Rialto which he took around the various meetings, riding it himself with great success.

The first meeting I went to was at Cessana, and almost the first person I ran into was Captain Mewburn. 'You're just the bloke I want to see,' was his greeting. 'You remember that horse you helped me to christen?' I did. A beauty he was an Arab stallion, pure white; the Captain had been very excited about it when he got him, had told me he was going to race him and asked

153

me what I thought he ought to call him. I looked him over. 'Why not White Bollocks?' I said. 'I don't think that that would look too good on the card. I'll tell you what though, I'll call him Silver Stones, that's near enough isn't it?' Anyway it appeared that Captain Mewburn had got this Silver Stones entered at Cessano in the five furlong sprint but hadn't got a jockey for it, and wanted to know whether I'd be prepared to ride him. I agreed, and it seemed I'd started something for he went on about one of his sergeant's horses, Tamara. 'He's blind in one eye, but he's a bloody good jumper. We've been schooling him. Will you ride him over the fences?' I told the captain about my experience with St Andrew and how I didn't fancy going through that again. 'But you're just the sort of rider he needs,' he said, and I allowed myself to be persuaded.

It could only have been a minute after I'd left the captain when I thought I saw a face I recognized. 'It couldn't be,' I said to myself, for it was sticking out of a captain's uniform, but it was, and seconds later I was shaking hands with Ray Groombridge, who'd been stable lad under me just before the war. 'Captain Ray bloody Groombridge,' I almost yelled, 'Well, well, well.' He looked a bit embarrassed. 'Luck of the draw, Phil' he said, but I later found out it wasn't. He'd gone abroad to Iraq with a cavalry regiment early on in the war and had earned each promotion. 'I've got Wilf Parkes with me, he's my staff sergeant.' Wilf Parkes was another stable lad, who'd been apprenticed to Tom Walls, the actor, owner and trainer. He and I used to do the washing-up together when Tom Walls gave parties at his house in Epsom, right orgies we used to think them. He was one of my greatest pals and had been best man at my wedding. This meeting was proving as social as Derby day. It also proved what I said at the beginning of this chapter, that square pegs didn't have to stay in round holes, that anyone prepared to use his loaf could sort out a job where he was best able to serve both his country and himself.

Ray and Wilf naturally wanted to know if I had any likely winners so I tipped them my two. When Ray heard I was riding, he asked me if I knew anything about mules. I told him I did. 'There's a corporal Machin got one, a great big bugger and he's looking for someone to ride it over fences today, will you take it on?' That was three rides in one afternoon, it seemed I was as

154

much in demand as Gordon Richards. Fortunately I was wearing the uniform breeches and putties and I'd chanced my arm by coming along in my jodhpur boots which had travelled through Africa and Italy with me and were more comfortable than the Army issue, so I only had to change into the colours that were provided. My first race was on Silver Stones. Captain Mewburn was the starter so naturally he put me in the best position on the rails. 'Give me the nod when you're ready, Phil, then I'll let 'em go.' This I did and got away to a fine start, kept ahead of the field and won with ease, with my new-found pals cheering me on and congratulating me on the money I'd won them. It was the same with the chase and one-eyed Tamara, there was no holding him, he cantered in. Again the lads were ecstatic and started singing that old army song, 'Look what he did with the one-eyed Riley, boom, boom, boom,' etc.

When I went to the start on my next mount, the big Algerian mule, I found I'd been made favourite. It was tote betting, but apparently most of the money was on me. All very flattering but a bit of a responsibility. Both the equipment and the technique of riding these animals were different. Riders didn't have a saddle, just an ordinary army blanket folded in four with a surcingle round it to tighten it into position, and a bridle. You sat on the mule's behind, not on the withers. It looked funny, just like those shots on the movies when Arabs ride donkeys, but it's right and proper and that way you can do anything with them. Corporal Machin gave me some instructions, he also pushed a couple of drawing pins half into the heels of each of my boots and pulled the heads outwards. 'Give 'im a dig with these when you come to a fence. He likes a bit of encouragement, you'll find they're as good as spurs.' It was bending the rules a bit but nobody was any the wiser. Though the animal went well and did as he was told, I'm afraid I disappointed the punters by finishing fourth.

This was the first of many enjoyable days I spent racing in Italy. I didn't always ride, but I mixed with the boys who did and shared any information that was going. I'm afraid the regulations weren't as strict as they were in England, and Lady Luck hadn't much of a part to play, for many of the races were fixed and most of the others were racing certainties. As a consequence even I went mad with my money and built up what was to me a small fortune. Your ordinary Tommy Atkins racegoer, however,

155

was nobody's fool, for while he may not have felt that the results were a foregone conclusion, he did notice that most of the blokes that were collecting from the tote were members of the Veterinary Corps or chaps like myself in riding breeches and wearing yeomanry cap badges. They took to standing next to the tote window and when we went up to place our bets their ears would be flapping and a couple of minutes later they'd follow suit. This cheating practice became so common that it affected the eventual payout adversely and it was decided amongst ourselves that something had to be done about it. The plan we made was simple, we either borrowed or hired a side cap from a bloke from another regiment or even swopped with some innocent on the course. Both schemes worked well, particularly the swopping since by following him the smart boys were following the bets of a mug punter with the inevitable consequences.

So I spent my last working and leisure hours in the army with four-legged creatures, doing the things I enjoyed and was trained to do. Eventually my demob group came close enough for me to allow myself to look forward to returning home. It was now that I realised my newfound wealth was a bit of an embarrassment. It was allied currency which had no value at home. I tried to change some at the NAAFI at a hell of a loss, but as the time grew nearer I knew I should still have a deal left over. In desperation I tried exchanging it through the usual channels but the first question I was asked was, 'How did you come by it?' and when I explained that I'd won it racing, I got the same kind of treatment as you'd get from an incometax inspector at home. Eventually I was giving it away, but even that wasn't easy.

In case I've been sounding a bit like a Scrooge, let me say that by the time I got on the plane to come back home, all thoughts of money had left me and when finally I was through the demob centre at Guildford and on course for home, I reckoned I had cause to be grateful. I'd had a good war, led an interesting life, met a lot of bloody good blokes, seen a bit of the world and got through without a scratch. It couldn't be bad.

9

The old routine – Wallington's war – Goodbye Welsh the fish-monger – Changing attitudes of stable lads – Tinker Tailor owners – Alligator Satinoff – Icecream and horses: the Pacito Brothers – Dave Morris and the Falcon Pipe – Tom Olson and Fullshaw Cross – The Manchester United air crash hits our stable – In the doldrums – Taking time with Hasty Cloud – We win the Cambridgeshire at last – The death of Harold Walling-ton – Young Harold moves over – A new style – The tax man closes in – Death duties kill the work of a lifetime – Postcript: in trouble with the stewards – Seeing my time out with my four-legged friends

It was strange going back into the racing world after being away for six years. Many of the old faces were missing, and some of the new ones didn't seem to fit. The war had had a real meaning for me. It was difficult to replace this and to return to the racing scene with my previous enthusiasm. Somehow the whole business seemed to have got smaller. Cath must have sensed what I was feeling, for she tried every means she could to persuade me to give the game up. I wouldn't have been alone. Many found they could get better-paid jobs with sociable hours offering, as they thought, greater opportunities. I believe that if my home hadn't been in Epsom and I hadn't had Harold Wallington on my doorstep and I hadn't smelt the stables, I might have allowed myself to be persuaded. As it was, it was all too easy to slip back into the old routine and as everyone around me seemed anxious to forget the war, to allow it to become almost a dream.

With the closing of race courses and with petrol rationing which affected the transporting of animals for any distance,

Harold had realized that if he was to survive as a trainer he would have to move to an area where racing was zoned. He decided on Malton in Yorkshire, where he shared stables with H. Bellerby. I suppose like others who continued training during the war, the best that could be said about them was that they survived. Harold had one or two useful horses like Emolument, Patricia Ann and Fragrant View, but there weren't the opportunities to exploit them fully. I think it might well have been touch and go whether he would have been able to continue after the war if Lady Luck hadn't smiled on him. As it was he was able to return to Epsom with an even greater prize than St Andrew had been. This time it wasn't a horse, it was an owner, a Mr Willie Satinoff, a wealthy manufacturing tailor from Manchester. It was he who gave Harold his enthusiasm for the future, some of which brushed off on to me.

Once Cath had accepted my return to the horses, our life together settled down happily. There was only one blot on the horizen, mum had been a war casualty. Like most cockney families, she and dad had refused to allow the Germans to shake them. They had the money to move into the country, but they never considered leaving. The business thrived, what dad lost through shortages of fish, potatoes and oil, he made up with his dealings in the black market. By that I don't mean that he was a spiv, but he took advantage of whatever he could lay his hands on, and Billingsgate market provided many opportunities of buying and selling other things apart from fish. He was no better or worse than most of his colleagues in this.

South-East London was on the receiving end of a large number of bombs and there were regular raids, particularly at night. Neither mum nor dad would consider the shelter, early on they decided that if they were going, they'd go in the privacy of their own home. One night there was a particularly heavy raid. Dad was in the local pub and thought it was more pleasant to sit it out there. Mum wandered into the street to see what was going on. A passing warden saw her and pushed her back indoors. I believe it was his last action on earth for seconds later a bomb fell a few doors down. The shutters of our shop took most of the force of the blast as they caved in, so although mum was bowled over she wasn't hurt. She picked herself up and went towards the living-room. Unfortunately the bomb had dislodged the old station-

158

type clock we had hanging on the wall and as mum passed it, it fell on her head, causing a nasty gash. She bathed it and by the time dad came back it had stopped bleeding and she made light of it. Despite her protests that there were many worse off than she was, dad took her to a first aid post where her wound was dressed and she was told to report to hospital the next day. She didn't, she found she had better things to do. Eventually the gash healed and she thought no more about it.

Some months later her memory started to fail her and her eyesight became affected. When I came back home, I could see that she had changed, but I didn't realise how serious her condition was until I caught her trying to read the paper upside-down. It could only have been a week or two after that that she had to go into hospital for a brain operation from which she never recovered. She died in September 1946. Six months later dad was forced to admit that the firm of Welsh had lost its senior partner. He made the worst possible decision and sold up and retired. That he was able to live well until he died in 1959 shows the kind of money he'd earned and saved, but from the moment he stopped working he was like a ship without a rudder. Cath and I tried having him to live with us, but it didn't work, he had to be master of his own destiny and he couldn't compromise.

As I became more familiar with the post-war racing scene, it became clear to me that the changes that had taken place were here to stay, and that there were many others on the way. Trainers now had to look for labour, and it wasn't cheap, though it was still low-paid compared with other jobs. Time was becoming money, the war had changed labour relationships, blokes weren't prepared to be spoken to roughly, nor were they prepared to work long and hard to learn their job. Feed for the horses was still scarce, which sent the prices soaring.

Perhaps the biggest change was in the type of owner now being attracted into racing. Before the war we had coined a phrase 'a tinker tailor owner'. He was something of a rarity, a working-class man who'd made some money and wanted to satisfy his lifelong amibiton of owning a race horse. He was generally a shop-keeper or publican or small businessman. He wasn't trying to better himself socially by getting on term with the gentry, he had a genuine interest in the game. He enjoyed showing his horse off to his pals and came to the stable more often than other owners. Stable lads were always glad to see him for he was generally free with his money. He'd come up the hard way himself, so knew that it was the lad at the bottom of the ladder who was doing the real work and that it was money well spent to see that he was kept happy. He was also able to be on terms with both the lads and the trainers like Herbert and Harold, who were chips off the same block. Your dukes, lords and gentry with their 'jolly good show' and 'well done, my man' may have contributed a good deal to racing, but they weren't any use to the boys. As one Australian lad I knew put it, after he'd been patronized and given nothing at the end of it, 'The trouble with those bastards is that they've got black adders in their fucking pockets.'

It now became apparent that there were going to be many more of these 'tinker, tailor' owners come into racing, that they wouldn't be content with just one horse, and that they would work as hard at the game as they had to accumulate the money they were investing in it. I think Harold was one of the first to recognize this change and to set about turning it to his own ends.

Once I had settled into stables Harold and I had to agree on exactly what my job was going to be. Before the war we just mucked along together with me acting as jack of all trades, treated as Harold's right-hand man, but still turning a hand to anything and everything, and in particular acting as stable lad to St Andrew. At Malton, he'd got a few lads together. I now felt it only right that I should be given a position where my duties were defined. Harold would have preferred to have carried on as before, but the army had given me a sense of authority, so I was determined and I got my way. I was now promoted to head travelling lad, which means what it says, that I was responsible for getting horses to meetings and seeing that they were looked after when they got there. I was on a par with the head lad, though my job suited me better for I enjoyed travelling around and was also in a good position for seeing how the horses performed, for having my small gamble and collecting from an owner who had a winner, while the iron was hot.

While he was in the north, Harold had met more of these 'tinker, tailor' owners, though with a difference. They were men who from small beginnings had built up big businesses, some of them as a result of the war. There were those who had gone into racing for prestige, others who had used it as a way of advertising their products, and those who saw it as a means of making money. I'm not sure why Mr Satinoff had first been attracted to it, but I do know that he stayed in it for the last two reasons. He was a manufacturing tailor. He made clothes for both men and women and he sold wholesale to the shops. He made the same articles of clothing for a variety of stores but they were given different labels and different prices, although it appeared that they'd been specially made for one. He also marketed some articles under his brand name 'Alligator', which was why many of his horses were given names like Brown Alligator, Flying Alligator and Merry Alligator. If he had a winner, shop windows would display a blown-up picture of the horse finishing with the caption 'Alligator leads the field'.

Harold and Satinoff hit it off immediately. They were both in racing for the money they could make from it and once they realized that each could trust the other to play his part, they entered into an agreement that was only broken by death. Although they worked closely together and Satinoff was consulted at every stage, he was sensible enough to leave the decisions concerning training, racing and running of the horses with Harold. He provided the money, which wasn't difficult for his early successes made racing self-financing for him. Although I believe he had a real affection for horses, he looked on them mainly as money machines.

Most of the races they ran in were at the smaller meetings, where an entry by Satinoff and Wallington would set bookies' hearts beating faster and their minds puzzling whether it was today that this partnership had decided to have it off or not. To the lads he was the ideal owner, for not only was he free with his money but also provided them with clothes. An invitation to his store in London meant a new jacket or pair of trousers as well as money for a good meal and tickets to a show. Once when I went there, to be fitted for a new suit, his head man asked if I had a likely winner for that afternoon. It so happened I did, and at a very good price. Everyone there had money on it and it duly obliged at 100–8. Their delight and generosity knew no bounds and I went away with new everything, indeed I'm wearing the overcoat they gave me to this day, and it has a Moss Bros label sewn into it.

Other 'tinker, tailor' owners were the Pacito brothers, Alf and Ernie, British-born Italian ice-cream merchants, with their shops along the front at Redcar, Scarborough and other Yorkshire resorts. Lady Luck was good to them. Mid View won the Zetland Gold Cup at Redcar and Alf's Caprice the Victoria Cup twice at Hurst Park. When I took two horses up to Redcar for the Easter meeting on the Saturday and Monday, I was given the freedom of the ice-cream parlours as well as dinners with the families. To the disgust of the lad who went with me Croppy Warrall, I got hooked on knickabocker glories. 'If you'd flavour the buggers with hops, I might have one,' he kept telling the waitresses. The Pacitos were a very popular family locally. They were grateful to have been given a home and the opportunity to make a good living in Britain, and showed it through their generosity. This kind of popularity had its disadvantages, for even if their horses ran down south, all the punters around would back them and they'd be returned at shorter prices than they deserved. This was confirmed to me by a local barber who asked me if I had any tips for the Easter meeting. 'You could do worse than back the Pacito's two,' I told him. 'No point in that, half the town will be on them, they'll be no price at all.' As it happened, Doug Smith rode Mid View and Top Drawer to victory for them, which bears out the old saying, 'it's better to have short price winners than long price losers'.

Mr Raine was another small owner who made and distributed cheese. Although he only had a couple of horses, he was worth a lot to the lads. He didn't seem to know the difference between a quid or a fiver. We also found ourselves advertising pipes through Mr Dave Morris. John Beary, his previous trainer at Lambourne, died and as Morris' business was now mainly conducted in London, he wanted his horses nearer home. He had previously won the Cambridgeshire with Loppy Lugs, but we also did exceptionally well for him, at a time when our stables were in need of a life line. I collected two of his horses, one of which was called Tandia. We'd only had him a short time when he won the London Cup at Alexandra Park. As a result Mr Morris bought two yearlings and they were given to us to look after. When the time came to name them, he called one of them Falcon Hunter, which struck me as peculiar as it bore no relation to the names of either the dam or sire. It turned out that Mr

Morris owned the Falcon Pipe Company, manufacturing a new kind of pipe for wet smokers which you could buy with a change of bowl. I was, however, a bit upset when a week after Tandia won another race, Harold told me that his name was to be changed to Feuedor. 'Why, it's a bloody stupid name,' I said. 'It's also dangerous. Change yer name, change yer luck.' It appeared that it was being done for business reasons. Mr Morris had just bought the British rights of a new kind of lighter by the name of Feuedor. I don't know if unplaced horses are a good advertisement, I wouldn't have thought so, but I was right in my gypsy's warning. The horse never won again.

I liked Dave Morris. He was more the old-fashioned type of owner who loved his horses, win or lose, and who often insisted on running them just for the fun of it. He was a great friend of the boxing promotor Harry Levine, and the pair of them would visit us together. This again was good for the lads for though he had no cause to, Harry would always give them a drink. I was eventually able to repay Mr Morris for his kindnesses. It was when I became head lad for Wallington and Mr Bertie Kerr sent us five yearlings to find owners for. As it happened, Alf Pacito was the first to see them, though he was a bit dubious about taking on any more since his brother was having eye trouble. There was one that I thought stood out, it was later called Juke Box, and I urged him to buy it. He finally came out against it, so when a few days later Dave Morris came down, I recommended the colt to him and he bought it.

Juke Box did splendidly, ending up by winning the Spillers Stewards Cup at Goodwood against all the odds, for he was drawn number one, the worst possible position and carried top weight. We were lucky though to have Lester Piggot riding for us; our chances which had been halved by the draw were now doubled. Not long after this success, Juke Box was sold to stand at stud in Ireland. The price paid was in the region of £10,000 and again whoever bought him got a bargain for he's been one of the most successful sires in that country.

Not all our owners were in trade. Tom Olson was one of the exceptions, he was brother of Sir Eric Olson, owner of the Derby winner, Dante. I don't know how he and Harold got together, the first I heard of it was when I was asked to pick up a yearling filly from a Newbury stud farm, and a very humbling experience it turned out to be. I arrived there in the afternoon. No one was there except a knarled old groom. He was expecting me and showed me to the box where the yearling was. I put a bridle and a lead rein on her with this old chap watching me, a bit critically I thought, and he began irritating me. So when he asked if I wanted any help boxing her, I treated him short. 'No, no need for that, I've boxed hundreds in my time. There's no reason for you to hang around.' He sloped away and I walked the horse towards the box. The driver had got the ramp down ready for her to go in but she took one look at it and stopped. She stood stone still and nothing I could do would budge her. She wasn't playing up, nothing awkward about her, she just wouldn't move either backwards or forwards into it. I tried every trick I knew and talked myself hoarse trying to persuade her.

The box driver began to get irritated and impatient. 'We'll have to leave the bloody thing. I'll go and ring the guv'ner and tell 'im we can't box 'er.' This would have meant defeat. ''ang on a minute, I'll give her one more try,' I said. Just at that moment, the little gnome of a stud groom appeared from nowhere in his old smock coat. I reckon he must have been watching us all the time. 'You two still here? You seem to be in some difficulty: What's the trouble?' I told him shirtily that I couldn't get the bugger into the box. 'That's strange,' he said, 'she's always been as good as gold. 'ere, give 'er to me.' He took off the bridle, put the rein on the head collar, then he started talking to her. 'Come on, old girl, now don't let's have no bother, you show them how good you are.' He then walked up the ramp and into the box with the bloody animal following him. I stood there gaping, feeling no end of an ignorant fool. 'You won't be needing me any more now, gents, so I'll wish you good afternoon,' the groom said as he disappeared as quickly as he'd come.

Fullshaw Cross, for that was the name she was given, turned out to be a real goodun. I broke her in and decided to look after her, for I hadn't got a horse at the time. To coin a phrase, she was a most gentlemanly lady, it was exactly like dealing with someone of good birth. She won many races, including the Crocker Butell Handicap at Hurst Park. Scobie Breasley always rode her and well except in her most important race, the Parkhill Stakes at Doncaster, where she ran second to the world beater, Petite Etoile. It was everyone's opinion in our stable that she should have won. When Tom Olson originally engaged Scobie as a jockey, I heard him say to him, 'If you ride her as I tell you to ride her and get beaten, I shan't say a word, but if you try anything different, I shall be very angry.' Not that I think Scobie tried anything different on this occasion, he was noted for racing among the pack and with his superb judge of pace going away when it looked as if his horse was beaten. This time he left it seconds too late, he misjudged both Petite Etoile and her jockey, Lester Piggot, and was beaten narrowly. Tom Olson was raging mad and to his dying day swore he'd been robbed of the race. He had cause to be grateful to the horse, though, for when he sold her he got a high price.

He spent part of the money on another yearling, a filly with the same grandparents as Fullshaw Cross. It's only natural that I should expect as well-behaved a horse but Downhill Only was mischievous. She had plenty of guts but if any animals came near her she'd squeal and kick at them. So it was that she and Tom Olson got some compensation for her relation's defeat at Doncaster when she ran in the Singleton Handicap at Goodwood. Natural, the Duke of Norfolk's horse, was, it seemed, every punter's choice and was short-priced favourite. When all the runners were at the starting gate, Burns, first jockey to the Duke, walked his animal up behind Downhill Only and Natural was given a nasty kick for her pains. The vet looked at her, but pronounced her fit to race. That was as maybe, but our filly skated in and the favourite was nowhere, and it was everyone's opinion that Downhill Only was to blame. Tom Olson was the right kind of owner, a man who loved horses, knew a deal about them so that while he was able to leave the day-by-day routine to the stables, he was able to make his contribution in the placing and running of them. He had good connections in the racing world, and I think that he and Harold might eventually have scaled the heights together if it hadn't been for his untimely death from a heart attack at one Epsom meeting.

In February 1958 came a tragedy that shocked the world and which had a disastrous effect on our stables. It was the Manchester United air disaster. It killed many members of the football team but another of the victims was Willie Satinoff. He'd been offered a place in the aircraft by one of United's directors. Although Mrs Satinoff had enjoyed racing, her pleasure from it came though her husband's success, so all the horses were sold and dispersed. Harold grieved first for the loss of a friend, but later, when he was able to assess the damage, the blow to the stables. It was as though he had lost his right arm as well as twelve horses.

Harold and Satinoff had made plans for the future, which could have lifted our stables into the top class. Having proved to himself that he could succeed in the racing world, with middle-class horses, Satinoff had been looking forward to progressing both as a breeder and in classic racing. He'd had a success with Castel Marina, a two-year-old in the Solario Stakes at Sandown. He was a colt he'd bred from a brood mare bought from Bertie Kerr in Ireland, and had pronounced in my hearing to Harold that they were now ready to go places together. It was the golden opportunity for any trainer, a man with money showing absolute trust and with the will to succeed. It was the chance of a lifetime, something that rarely ever happens twice. Now we had to keep going somehow.

The effect of Satinoff's death was noticeable in the number of winners we had during the year following. We dropped from around thirty to sixteen. It was lucky that one of these was the Royal Hunt Cup at Ascot with Faultless Speech, since this carried with it a deal of prestige. Although the stables eventually recovered, poor old Harold was never quite the same man, and I wish I had as many pound notes as the times he said to me, 'If Satinoff was alive today, we'd've done so and so.'

It was, I believe, a horse called Hasty Cloud that eventually re-established our reputation. He belonged to another 'tinker, tailor' owner, Mr Walters. He'd begun with a paper-shop in Luton, then as the population increased with the Vauxhall factory there, he expanded and made a lot of money, although he threw his cash around like a man with no arms. At the start we were not impressed with Hasty Cloud. 'Looks too big for my liking,' was the governor's comment, 'but let's hope he goes early for we need everything we can get, and this Walters can afford a few more. He just needs a little encouragement.' He kept the pot boiling by telling Walters that being a big-framed horse, he wouldn't be able to hurry him but that we hoped he'd be ready around half-way through the season. He wasn't, he was bloody useless, couldn't get out of his own way. It was no good entering him, he wouldn't have been able to perform at all. In desperation the governor decided to run him at the end of the season at the last Lingfield meeting, a seven furlong race for two-year-olds. All we could hope was that he'd be somewhere up with the field. There was no way he could win. He was as slow as he'd been at the beginning of the season.

It was a murky day matching Harold's and my spirits, when we set out for Lingfield, though we tried to put on a bit of a show for the owner's sake. To our delight the weather got worse, fog came down, you couldn't see a furlong, so racing was cancelled. Mr Walters wasn't pleased of course, but he left the horse with us during the winter. Came the spring, we began putting the young two-year-olds to work on the Downs and Harold came up to me and said, 'Phil, I want you to take Hasty Cloud out to lead them. He's a quiet enough horse and should behave well with them.' He was right there, he didn't seem to have a worry in the world, didn't mind them bumping into him and wasn't in the least bit coltish. He gave the impression he didn't know what it was for. After he'd led these two-year-olds about a month, Harold decided to gallop them with Hasty Cloud. Now, two-year-olds when they're young only know how to go fast, they jump off and race like hell, they haven't yet learned what is meant by being controlled. So off we set and I found Hasty Cloud was going like the clappers. After the gallop was over I rode up to the governor and told him that the horse had improved out of all recognition. He didn't believe me. 'But it's true,' I told him, 'If I'd given him a quick kick in the belly he'd have run away from them.' I was proved right when later they were given longer gallops. Hasty Cloud made hacks out of the two-year-olds, they couldn't get near him, couldn't blow wind up his arse as the saying goes. What had changed the horse I'll never really know, but I think that it was running with youngsters that did it. He wanted to show he was best.

Hasty Cloud won a number of races, including the Sandown Anniversary Cup and then the Norwich Handicap over a mile at Newmarket. It was the Cambridgeshire that was his race, though, he was second in 1962, third 1963 and finally won it in 1964. His successes were a great feather in Harold's cap and we were now back in full business again. Mr Walters gave us a couple more horses, one of them, Cresta Court began by winning two races on the trot. I suppose Walters must have been pleased, but he didn't show his appreciation in the usual way. When he died of a coronary, one of the lads remarked, 'It's certain it wasn't brought on by putting his hands into his pockets.'

Our stables now ran on a fairly level keel though there never has been nor ever will be anything predictable about racing. It was towards the end of the 1960s that Harold began showing signs of old age. If anything he grew more secretive, and though he pretended to be in the process of handing the reins over to his son, he just couldn't seem to bring himself to do it. This made my position as head lad more difficult. I didn't know who I was supposed to go to for instructions and often ended up making my own decisions. Young Harold was both irritated and confused. It was only when the governor had two illnesses that his son was able to come into his own and by the time Harold died in 1973, he was in command.

After his father's death we worked hard together and got on well. Young Harold attracted another kind of owner, his education had put him into a different class from his father, and he was able to be on easy terms with people of a different social world. The future looked bright. Then came the crunch. Harold had made no provision for his death so his estate became liable for heavy death duties, the tax men closed in and the stables had to be sold to pay whatever they said was owing. So, in 1974, Harold Wallington stopped existing as a training establishment. I stayed on with a lad, Paddy Fitzgerald, packing things up and selling off various items. I also now had time to think about what I was going to do myself. I had offers from other stables, but after 47 years in only two jobs, I was chary of jumping too suddenly into anything. I thought I'd give myself time to look around, so when I finally collected my cards on 31 December, 1974 I became unemployed for the first time in my life and my wife and I took a holiday together, again for the first time ever.

There is one event in my racing career that so far I haven't mentioned. I've left it till now because I think it has a particular significance when I come to look back over my time in stables. It happened in the early 1950s, the year Nick the Rocker won the Northumberland Plate. I was told by Harold to take Devon Cottage, one of Satinoff's horses, to Newcastle as he felt it was too long a journey for him just for one day's racing. I had a lad, Sonny Oxford with me, and when we got to the course and had done the horse over for the night, he asked me if he could stay with some friends of his in Gateshead, a nearby town. I agreed, though I was reluctant since we had Tom Mahon, an apprentice from Manton coming over early to give the horse an outing before the race. Sonny promised he wouldn't be late, so that was that.

The following morning I fed the horse around 5.30 a.m. and later went back into the yard to muck out and get him ready. Still Sonny wasn't back, so I went away for a cup of tea. When I returned he was there, putting the tack on the horse. He was chatting to a chap standing nearby, he didn't introduce me, so I thought he was just another trainer's lad. When we'd got the horse ready, we led him out of the yard and as we got to the gate, were stopped by the man on duty who asked if we'd signed the book. I had, so had Sonny, but this other lad who was still with us, hadn't. Nor had he got a card allowing him in. It turned out that when Sonny had come in, he'd brought his pal with whom he'd spent the night. There'd been no-one on the gate when they'd arrived and he'd invited him to have a look at our horse. This was, of course, strictly against the rules. I gave them both a rollocking, apologised to the man on the gate and thought no more of it.

Later that day, just before the first race, I went to the Clerk of the Course's office and declared Devon Cottage as a runner. I'd only just moved away when I heard over the tannoy, 'Will Mr Wallington's representative please report to the Clerk of the Course's office,' so back I went, to be told that I was up before the stewards at 2.30. Before that time Mr Satinoff had arrived and I told him my news. I was still not sure what it could be about, I couldn't believe that it was to do with the early morning incident in the stable. At the appointed time I went along with Mr Satinoff. He waited outside when I was called in. There were three stewards sitting at a table. It was about the morning's incident, so I told them my story truthfully. They didn't look impressed, they cross-examined me, tied me in knots and then asked if there was anyone at the meeting who could vouch for me. I called Mr Satinoff, he spoke highly of me and of the years I'd been in racing. That seemed to make matters worse. 'With that kind of service, he should have known better than to have allowed a stranger into the stables.' They told Satinoff he could leave, got off their chairs, went into a huddle in the corner of the room, came back and the chief steward looked me straight in the eyes and said, 'We have no alternative but to fine you twenty-five guineas.' His verdict bowled me over. At that time it was big money. 'I'm sorry, sir,' I said 'but I can't pay.' 'In that case we have no option but to warn you off.' I then thought of Mr Satinoff outside, and asked if I could speak to him. He quickly gave me the money, I was given a receipt and that was the end of the matter as far as they were concerned. For me it was a deep and wounding blow. I believed I'd been treated roughly and unfairly. It was months before I could put the incident in the back of my mind.

But today I'm able to say that the stewards were right. Stewards are there to see that the standards of British racing are upheld. They've done it well over the years when other sports have changed beyond recognition, and now hardly deserve to be called the name. Their reason is not difficult to see, having made the rules they come down hard when an offender is found out. To them the game is bigger than the individual, so the punishment they hand out, while it may seem hard, is given not as a revenge for a wrong, but as a warning to others who may be considering stepping out of line. They're not prepared to accept excuses or what are called mitigating circumstances. They can see all too clearly what leniency can lead to. So, my final words on racing must be, leave them alone. They've run it successfully for years, let them continue to do so.

Being out of work and on the dole when I was 59 didn't appeal to me. I felt a sponger going down to the Labour Exchange to collect my dues. They made things as easy for me as they could there, but obviously they'd no jobs on offer that had to do with horses. I had one or two enquiries from local trainers, but having been in the position of head lad for many years, I couldn't see myself taking orders from younger and less experienced blokes. I was getting a bit desperate sitting round the place doing nothing. I was used to rising early and the days seemed to get longer. An Epsom meeting gave me the chance to pull out of my depression. I dressed up in my gear and wandered onto the course. There were the usual greetings from my mates and from trainers and jockeys, but they seemed to be tinged with pity, as though I was an old horse, past his best, just a hack. Backing a couple of losers didn't help, and I was about to make off home when I ran into someone I'd known most of my life, Brigadier Green, a steward and in charge of the Apprentice School at Goodwood. He gave me the friendliest welcome of the day. 'Hallo, Welsh, good to see you. In fact, I think you may be just the man I'm looking for. I understand you're not working at the moment.' I told him he was right on that score. 'Well, would you consider coming to me. I'm running racecourse security for the Southern Region and I'm in need of people who know the game to help me,' he said, then added with a twinkle, 'set a rogue to catch a rogue, eh?' We talked about what the work entailed, and the following week I went to see him to have the job fully explained and I enlisted.

Now, obviously, I can't talk about my work, otherwise it would cease to be security. I'm not a Sherlock Holmes or a Sexton Blake, but it's interesting. I travel around a lot and once again I'm with horses and the people who care for them, and if I keep a clean crime sheet and a civil tongue in my head, it's how I hope to see my working life out. It's as fitting an ending as I could have wished for.

That then brings me to the end of my story. I began my working life in what was then the sport of kings, but has now perhaps become the industry of kings, so vast are the sums involved in breeding, racing and training. As I've said before, I've enjoyed every minute of it, though I've had to defend it against my wife and family. Perhaps it has been a selfish life from their point of view; every day, year in year out, horses have had to be looked after, so that my social life and theirs has been dictated by the horses' needs. I've had to dig my way through the snow to get to stables on Christmas Days. When I bought my first car and Cath grumbled, 'A lot of good that will be to us', she was right. On lovely summer days when other people were driving to the coast, I'd have to go to stables to feed and water horses, and I used to say to them, 'If it wasn't for you long-faced buggers I'd be on the beach now.' Cath has begged me countless times to get another job, and when I've countered with, 'What else can I do?' she's reeled off a dozen things. Still, I've always had the last word. 'I understand horses. There's nobody can tell me anything about them so there's no one better at their job than I am,' and to me this explains everything. It's the full circle. If you're good at it, you enjoy it. If you enjoy it, you're good at it. It's not just conceit, it's been my life's purpose.

Index